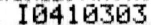

# FAITH IN THE FILIPINO

## THE RIPENING REVOLUTION

BY

## RAUL S. MANGLAPUS

Author of "FREEDOM, NATIONHOOD, & CULTURE"

A collection of speeches, statements and other public papers from 1959 up to the present of a former secretary of foreign affairs. His famous 1939 oration is included in the book together with the article specially written for and which appeared in "Foreign Affairs", a magazine published by the Council on Foreign Relations Inc. New York. His statement made on a paper defended by Arthur Schlesinger Jr. at a conference attended by both in Berlin has also been added.

Original Edition, 1961
Reissue, 2017

# ABOUT THE AUTHOR

Raul Manglapus y Sevilla is known for many things.

At the age of 38 he was the youngest Filipino ever to hold the Office of Secretary of Foreign Affairs. At 35 he already held under the Magsaysay administration the very sensitive end demanding office of Foreign Affairs Under-secretary.

Since then, even as a private citizen, he has been Invited by the governments of nations in six continents to speak before their peoples. At the 1960 Congress for Cultural Freedom In Berlin, be gave a much-applauded reply to a paper defended by United States Presidential Adviser Arthur Schlesinger Jr. At a 1961 meet in New Delhi, he delivered a brilliant dissertation on Asia's capacity for democracy.

He was graduated *summa cum laude* from the Ateneo de Manila, the school which produced Jose Rizal, Gregorio del Pilar, Antonio Luna, Claro M. Recto.

Manglapus is also known as a song-writer. A record of six of his well-known marches, sung by Aurelio Estanislao and Rene Antonio, has just been released.

Manglapus' record during the war is outstanding. Proving that his nationalism is one of deeds and not of words, he preferred torture and imprisonment in Fort Santiago to collaborating with the enemy. He later escaped to join the guerrillas in the hills, fighting with them and cheering them with his songs.

Manglapus is perhaps best known as a speaker and speech writer. The Philippines first heard him in 1939 when he represented the Ateneo de Manila in an inter-university oratorical contest. President Quezon, who was present as guest of honor, was so impressed with the young student's eloquence and with written speech that thenceforth he began to call on him for advice whenever Presidential speeches were to be made before youthful audiences. Since then Manglapus has been much in demand as a speaker here and abroad. The sparkling wit and impelling logic of his speeches, delivered in a number of languages and several Philippine dialects, have won over a great variety of audiences.

But more important perhaps than all these distinctions, what In fact makes these accomplishments possible and gives them meaning, is Manglapus dedication to two basic idea — faith in the Filipino and the necessity of decentralizing political and economic power. Those two Ideas form the basic philosophy of this book, the two motifs making up the theme which runs through the speeches, talks and statements collected here.

The last paragraph of Fr. Horatio de la Costa's foreword for Manglapus' first book of speeches, *Freedom, Nationhood and Culture,* is just as applicable to this book:

"On all or most of these questions Mr. Manglapus has something relevant to say. The trouble is, that with questions of such fundamental import, it is difficult to be relevant without being also dull. I suppose that Is why practised speech-makers prefer to be merely witty about them. But wit is often most effective when it is most irrelevant; and even at best, it is a lightning flash, a momentary illumination which leaves the darkness deeper than before. It is greatly to Mr. Manglapus' credit that between the lightning flashes of his wit he provides us with the humbler hut steadier light of reasoned argument."

----

## Dedicated to the memory of Ramon Magsaysay, the ripening of whose magnificent revolution we are seeking to speed.

----

# FOREWORD

In 1939, Raul S. Manglapus delivered an oration at an inter-university oratorical contest entitled "Land Of Bondage, Land Of The Free". President Manuel L. Quezon, who was present as the guest of honor, was deeply impressed by it. The oration has now become a classic.

Manglapus indicted a system which kept the tao in political and economic bondage in spite of constitutional assurances of liberty. In his peroration, he foretold an aimed peasant revolution if the causes of discontent which he had enumerated were, not promptly removed.

The causes were not removed. Six years later his prophecy came true. The peasant struck in Central Luzon. The tragedy was compounded by the fact that the Communist Party succeeded in seizing the leadership of the revolution.

To quell the uprising, Ramon Magsaysay put new spirit in the Philippine Army. To prevent a recurrence, he began his own revolution.

Twelve years after Manglapus had delivered his indictment and made his prophecy, Magsaysay began to remove the causes of discontent and to dignify the citizen in the barrio. Responding to the need of the hour, his revolution succeeded in turning the eyes of the people away from Mount Arayat and back to Malacanang.

# Faith in the Filipino

Malacanang was returned to the people and the people rejoiced. Yet, raising the hopes of the people and concentrating these hopes on his leadership was not to be the final destiny of the Magsaysay Revolution. He realized that perpetuating such a situation within the framework of an over-centralized government would merely mean that the faith of the citizen would be revived only to be smothered to death by a demoralizing dependence on an officious central government.

Thus Magsaysay sought, after turning the hopes of the citizen back to Malacanang, to turn it to the citizen's own self. Before his tragic death, he initiated a program which would mean the ripening of his revolution. The barrio citizens were at last to be given a just measure of self-government, the opportunity to develop their communities by their own effort and to permit their historical self-reliance to contribute its share to national development.

In political terms, this meant decentralization of government. In the economic field, this meant complete confidence in private initiative with government incentives. In sum, all this meant a revival of the Faith of the Filipino in himself.

He did not live to see the ripening. But a persistent group, the famous "young men" whom he had gathered around him to give vigor, vision and drive to his administration, today continue to fight for its realization.

Raul S. Manglapus, one of those men, is today perhaps the most articulate, logical and effective exponent of decentralization and private initiative in the Philippines.

What follows is a collection of his speeches from 1959 up to the present. To give the reader the fullest understanding of Mr. Manglapus' political thinking, the short talks given in Berlin and New Delhi, his statements, and other public papers in the same period have been added.

Included also is the article written upon the invitation of the editors of Foreign Affairs magazine which is reprinted here by special permission of its publislters, the Council On Foreign Relations Inc. New York.

This book is a sequel to Mr. Manglapus' first collection of speeches, "Freedom, Nationhood, and Culture" Published in 1959. His famous 1939 oration "Land of Bondage, Land of the Free" is also included as an appendix to complete the inspiring story of "Faith in the Filipino — The Ripening Revolution."

The original Publishers

# CONTENTS

# Faith in the Filipino

-----

*El dia en que el triunfo corone nuestros
ideales, el dia en que la republica brille en los
horizontes espanoles, tendremos ocasion de im-
plantar una reforma amplia, una ley municipal y
provincial altamente radical, democratica con vida
propia, independiente y autonoma, cual cumple y
honra a nuestras conviciones republicanas.*

-----

The day that triumph shall crown our ideals,
the day that our republic shall shine in Hispanic
horizons, we shall have occasion to implant ample
reforms — a truly radical law for the provinces and
municipalities, which shall have their own democratic
existence, independent, and autonomous,
in keeping with our republican convictions.

— Graciano Lopez Jaena
Barcelona, 1891

...this is of natural right, and nature itself enjoins it even on brute animals. Thus we see that cranes, ants and sheep have governors and chiefs belonging to their respective species and not to others; and St. Thomas shows that the head must be homogeneous with the body, tliat is, of the same nature. . .the magistrate should he familiar with the laws, customs, uses and abuses of his community, and this the alcalde mayor cannot be. because he has to depend on an interpreter, and if the interpreter is a native he has no command of Spanish, whereas if he is a Spaniard he understands the native but ill. And so even with the best of intentions he is liable to commit serious errors to the scandal of the natives, who see only what is done and not what is intended. It follows from this that alcaldes mayores are not qualified to attend to the details of administration. Let them leave these matters to the native magistrate, who without incurring the expense of hiring interpreters and scribes, but solely by word of mouth, can administer them better than the alcalde mayor with his interpreters and scribes, because of his familiarity with local conditions.

The Synod of Manila. 1581

-----

# I. Democracy and Windmills

(Speech delivered at the Commencement Exercises,<br>De La Salle College, March 15, 1959)

I am strongly reminded, because of the rather unique circumstances under which I find myself here today, of a story which was related to me about the Prime Minister of Australia when I was in that Continent last year. The Prime Minister, Mr. Menzies, a strict Presbyterian, was invited two years ago to the inauguration of St. Edmund's College, a new Christian Brothers' school in Canberra, the capital of the Australian Commonwealth. Mr. Menzies, whose excellent sense of humor is internationally known, began his speech in mock serious tones. Addressing himself to the Archbishop of Canberra, he said, "Your Craoe, I know not in truth why I am here. I'll have you reminded, sir. I'm a damned heretic."

I might, with perhaps graver reason, adopt the Prime Minister's attitude this afternoon and address myself thus to Brother Director: "Very Reverend Brother, I feel I must remind you, sir, I am a damned Blue Eagle."

It was in fact strongly suggested by some friends concerned for my health that I should not dare to make an appearance in this rostrum without bringing my anti-archer equipment.

But I refused to heed the solicitous suggestion. I thought my past and present associations with the faculty, alumni and student body of De La Salle College sufficiently warranted my coming here unarmored and unarmed.

The first leader that I ever chose to follow was a De La Salle alumnus, a spotless and fearless politician by the name of Lorenzo Tanada. And as if to return the compliment many of our staunchest and most uncompromising co-workers and supporters today are distinguished alumni of De La Salle.

In olden days there is said to have been a Philippine tradition regarding the choice of a career that parents might make for their children. If the child displayed a quick mind and facile tongue, he was made to take up law; if he was good at the use of his hands, he was made to take up surgery; if he was good at counting figures, he was made to take up business; if he was good at putting things together, he was made to take up engineering; if he was good for nothing in particular, then be was allowed to become a priest.

Fortunately, this tradition, if it ever in fact existed, has obviously changed. More and more of our most intelligent youth have chosen this most exalted of professions — the service of God.

But there was also another part of this tradition which went thus: if the child was quick at lying, was observed to be adept at purloining coins from his fathers pockets and was particularly adroit at making excuses, then there was only one career for him — politics!

The basic justification for this part of the tradition seems to be that politics being dirty, that politics being a jungle where only the wiliest and least principled can survive, then only the smart liar, the slippery thief, the smooth-tongued demagogue should be thrown into it. Keep the good boys out.

There is ample evidence, it would seem, to support this tradition. And there are many who are ready to accept it without protest.

But let us do a bit of analyzing and see where humor ends and truth begins.

What is politics? Is it what politicians make it? Or does it have an essence of its own? Webster defines it as the administration of public affairs in the interest of the peace, prosperity and safety of the state. And what is the rank of this calling among the vocations available to man? The answer comes from the Holy Father: no other calling is superior to politics save that of religion.

Let me first make it clear that I say these things not to inspire you to a career of politics. In truth, I should like to persuade you to the idea that politics is not a career for a few select members of the citizenry. It is rather as much a part of the essence of your lives, of the lives of each and every citizen as the eggs that you eat at breakfast and the shirt that you put on your back. It is so in a democratic society. It is only under a regime of tyranny that politics becomes the preserve of the chosen few.

Indeed, it has not always been so. Even the great French Revolution which occured in France only a few decades after the death of St. John Baptist de La Salle apparently did not contemplate such a radical situation as the sharing of the responsibilities of democracy by every citizen of the republic. The philosophers of the revolution, shocking as it may seem to those who now look up to them as the prophets of the inalienable rights of man, did not believe in equal rights for every man.

La Chalotais said: "The good of society demands that the knowledge of the common people reach no further than their immediate occupation. Any man who sees beyond his wretched trade will never acquit himself of his work with courage and patience. Among the common people no one needs to know how to read or write except those who live by those means."

But there was a group of men in France that believed otherwise, that believed in the right of every man, rich or poor, to be educated, to be able to reach the heights to which God had destined every man in a democratic state. These men were the Brothers of the Cliristian Schools.

La Chalotais, writing in his "Essai d'Education Nationale said. "The Brothers are ruining everything. They teach reading and writing to the people who ought never to learn anything but to draw and to handle the plane and the file." And Voltaire, enemy of the Church but supposed friend of democracy, said to him upon reading his essay, "I cannot thank you too much for giving me a foretaste of what you are about to give France. I find all your ideas useful. I am grateful to you for dissuading peasants from studying."

Were St. La Salle and his brothers ahead of their time? Perhaps. At any rate, it is this same belief in the right of every man to be educated, it is this same passion for universal education in duties of citizenship which St. La Salle preached in the face of those alleged rebels against tyranny, that today has become the cornerstone of every program for representative democracy. How curious that the program for the up-liftment and education of the *tao* in the barrio which Magsaysay began and could not finish, which some thought so radical and so new should find a parallel in the eighteenth century under such unexpected and conservative auspices as that of the Catholic order of the Christian Brothers.

Magsaysay wished to clean politics by rescuing it from the politician and placing it in the hands of the people. For this be wanted an educated and awakened citizenry. He wanted citizens everywhere, in the barrio as well as in the city, to think, to choose, to decide, to participate in the political life of the country. Here also was the desire of De La Salle — a desire so radical that even the supposedly violent revolutionary philosophers of his time like Rousseau and Voltaire believed it to exceed the ends of their revolution.

Here, indeed, is the challenge to the educated youth of a modem democracy: to make politics not so much a career but a part of their daily lives; to awaken to the reality that when they leave school they do not merely become members of an alumni association, of professional clubs, and of course of new families. They become members of a democratic society — a Christian democratic society in which their responsibility has increased precisely because they are educated.

The business of politics is your business as much as it is that of the career politician. It is your business particularly because you are a Christian. Thus, Cardinal Griffin told his English flock: "it is obvious that no Christian can declare that he is not his brother's keeper. We are members of one another. We are all brethren in Christ. It is unchristian therefore to imitate Pilate in washing our hands of public acts for which as members of the community we have a share of responsibility. If our rulers, acting in our name, do what is offensive to conscience, we must ask ourselves, "Who put these men in power?"

Indeed, my friends, when someone tells you of how corrupt some politicians are who ask "What are we in power for?", you might ask yourselves: "Who put these men in power?"

Wlio? It is he who could have been a good leader but chose instead to follow. It is he who could have followed a good leader but chose instead to follow anyone at all. These men are as guilty as the leader who is corrupt and as the men who chose to follow him.

Who are responsible for political confusion? For economic disorder? He, who having good ideas for economic progress, keeps these ideas to himself. He who has a choice of industries to pursue and chooses that which cannot help his country's economy. He who, having talent for organization, prefers to devote it to action irrelevant to the progress of his community. All these share in the responsibility for the confusion and the disorder with the demagogue, the incompetent representative of the people, the official who sits because of patronage and not of merit.

This, my friends, is politics — not just the election of men, not just the passing of laws, not just the enforcement of those laws. It is the total participation of the people in the affairs of the people. No one man can solve the problems of the people. This is the way of democracy, of a Christian democracy.

Is there a special challenge in all of this for the graduates of La Salle? There is. The original work of the La Salle brothers which began in the eighteenth century among the peasants of France is now expanded to embrace all levels of society. Here in the Philippines, the Christian Brothers are engaged in the education of young men from that segment of our society from which they are in a special position to lead. The evolution and the essence of the Brother's system of education, brought to bear upon the talent of these young men, produce citizens particularly prepared to be of great influence in the economic life and development of our country.

Will any one deny the urgency of the challenge of our times to these young men? The air is filled with the cry of economic independence. It is a good cry. It is only by heeding it that we shall give substance to the political independence that we now enjoy. But we cannot achieve that substance by quick, violent and ill-planned measures. It can be achieved only by the deliberate, relentless, intelligent planning and implementation by well-prepared citizens and agencies of the official and private sectors of our community.

Ultimately, it shall be the genius of young men like these graduates on which the country must depend for its salvation. But even as you go about the business of saving your country you will find that you will have a choice of paths to follow. You will find that in the name of patriotism there will be those who will come to you to convince you that the end justifies the means, that compromise of principles is acceptable when the end is such a glorious one as the salvation of your country. You will be offered positions of, falling down, you will adore the spirit of compromise and give up a few of the things you were told to hold sacred while you were in De La Salle. You will be asked to yield a little, to bend a little, to lie, to cheat, to bribe a little so that you may reach that position from which you might better help yourself, your family and your people.

If this should come to pass, you might recall that no country was ever saved by the spirit of compromise. The decay of every great society that has fallen began when its people accepted the spirit of compromise as part of the fabric of their civilization. Nations have never been saved by compromising statesmen. Such men have only succeeded in delaying their nations' doom. When nations have been saved at all it has always been by their own people who worked and planned and sacrificed and fought and died to keep their country strong and free.

Gentlemen of the graduating class, I have no doubt at all that in your time you will come upon the leadership of this nation. Then you shall have use for this thought: that in personal, in national and in international conduct, compromise is never good for anything but empty and temporary gain.

Many will taunt you to change your course. The established order within or the enemy without is too big to fight! Why challenge windmills? Why be a Don Quixote?

There was a contemporary of St. La Salle who answered this question. While St. La Salle was in Rheims plotting the course of his education campaign, this man was in Paris writing the most exquisite verses and fighting duels which monotonously ended in the demise of his adversary. His name was Cyrano de Bergerac.

To the exasperation of his enemies — and even of his friends — Cyrano consistently refused little compromises that could otherwise have improved his lot — could have enabled him to publish his verses, provided he allowed a prospective patron to change a line here and there, could have assured him a steady income provided he abandoned his gay independence and joined a nobleman's following.

One nobleman who was thus rebuked was tlie Count de Guiche. In the immortal, play by Edmond Rostand, de Guiche, despairing of Cyrano, asks him:

"Have you read Don Quixote?"

"I have," answers Cyrano, "and found myself the hero."

"Be so good as to read the chapter on the windmills."

"Chapter Thirteen."

"Windmills, you know, if you fight them . . . can cast you down into the mire!"

"Or", says Cyrano, "up among the stars!"

When you fight for your beliefs, you might, indeed, find yourself cast down into the mire. If so, you can always arise, brush off the mud and fight again. But there is always the chance that in the next charge you may find yourself swept up — among the stars.

That is the glorious promise of the fight for truth.

-----

# II. Optimism For Today

**(Speech delivered at the Centenary Homecoming, Ateneo Alumni Association, Loyola Heights, Quezon City. December 7. 1959)**

I was frankly surprised that I should be asked to address you at this centenary homecoming. Not having quite been blessed with success in a recent endeavor which was more or less of general knowledge, I did not feel qualified to sound the theme in an event so important in our nation's history as the 100th anniversary of the Ateneo de Manila. I was finally persuaded to accept the honor upon being informed by President Mering Ramos that I was indeed qualified for it because I am a "Great Atenean".

Now that it is all over, the story can be told. There is every truth to the canard so widely circulated during the campaign that the GA was only ostensibly the Grand Alliance and that in the secret code of the Black Pope it in fact meant the Great Ateneans. It was founded in fitting commemoration of the centenary of the founding of the Ateneo. All its founders were Ateneans. Pimentel. Manahan, Pelaez, Padilla, Rodrigo, Araneta and myself are alumni. Mondonedo is not an alumnus but he has one family circumstance of which he is proud or which he is still trying to live down (I know not exactly which) — his brother is a Jesuit. De la Rosa is not an alumnus but his children are in the Ateneo and in truth he is, of all of us, the closest to the Ateneo — he lives right across the street. Vargas is not an alumnus but he achieved national stature in Camp Murphy. And who is the patron saint in Camp Murphy? The very first GA in history — St. Ignatius Loyola!

This is a good time to answer the question: why were not Lacson, Quimson and Gene Magsaysay in the GA? Lacson, of course was an obvious sympathizer. But he never quite got to join the GA because he refused to be identified in the same political movement with Pimentel. Lacson has not yet forgiven Pim for killing him off in the first act of Cyrano de Bergerac in 1931. With his usual consummate modesty, Lacson explains that he had to get killed off because the script called for it but that (and I quote) "I can beat that bum in fencing anytime."

Quimson, as everybody knows, was really a GA fifth columnist in the Nacionalista ticket. He could not be accommodated in our ticket because although we had only six candidates the joint was not big enough for two or even one and a half Ilocano, and I am half Ilocano and I was there first, see? So we agreed that he would run in the Nacionalista ticket on one condition: If all GAs lost be would have to lose, too. And that is why as the count progressed and the GAs began to disappear in the horizon, Quimson had to maneuver it so that his votes were reduced. He ordered the bulk of his votes counted in favor of Pascual Racuyal.

As for Gene Magsaysay, I have only one explanation for his not joining the GA. In 1951 I taught Gene Political Law at the Ateneo Law School. In 1959 he deckled to run against me and show me he knew more about the subject than I did. I have the strangest feeling that he succeeded.

All this of course does not explain why the GA, having formed itself into a political movement, decided on such a difficult effort as to contest the two ruling parties without inspectors, without machinery and without sufficient funds. Some observers felt in the middle of the campaign that we were deliberately running to lose and not to win tlie elections. If this were true, then die story of the talking dog would seem to be in point:

One day a man bought himself a talking dog. He paid a very high price for it but he was confident that he could make more money taking bets on whether the dog could really talk or not. The man took the dog straight to the saloon where his gambling friends met and of course not one of them believed that it could talk. The man the confidently announced that he was willing to take bets. The odds went as high as 50 to 1 that the dog could not talk. The man took all bets. When the time came, the dog refused to talk. The man lost heavily.

Upon leaving the saloon, the man said to the dog: "Now look here, dawg, what'd you have to go and do that fer? Why did you refuse to talk? Do you realize how much money I lost on those bets?" The dog looked at the man winked at him and said: "Yeah. But think of the odds we'll get next time."

Gentlemen, you have our assurance that the CA fought to win, that it did not fight to lose and increase the odds on the betting in 61!

This is true, even if our cause seems to some cynics to be almost as impossible as a talking dog!

There are many explanations for our defeat and we must be grateful to ail those who have taken the trouble publicly to cushion its impact on the morale of the electors by analyzing the reasons for our lack of success in terms of a quick victory. Most of those are to be accepted as well founded. But there is one explanation which I cannot accept. It is that advanced by a few who are carried away by their strong sympathy for our cause and it runs as follows: The Filipino people are not ready for true democracy, our electorate is immature and unworthy of the right of suffrage.

I will not admit that our people are not ready for democracy. I will not admit that our electorate is extraordinarily immature. I will admit that we are asking too much of our people — which is not the same thing as saying that they are not worthy of the right of suffrage.

Yes, there are a big number of our people who vote by copying names mechanically from sample ballots. I said that immediately after elections and I say it again. We were not able to reach these people to explain our stand for lack of time and machine. Lacking any information on our position, lacking our sample ballots, they voted blindly for the names furnished them by the far reaching arms of the mighty party machines. It is not their fault that we did not reach them. Neither was it ours. Whose fault was it?

We are the only country in the world that requires our people to elect all the members of the senate at large. We are broken up into seven thousand islands at least four hundred of which must be visited if a national candidate is to explain his views properly to his electors. Transportation even in some parts of Luzon is extremely difficult. Some islands in the south still have sixteenth century roads. There are many towns that can only be readied by boat in Leyte, Samar and Cotabato. Many of the inhabitants in these towns are uninformed about national issues: they cannot be reached by the national candidate. But this does not make them immature or unprepared for democracy. It is just that the test for democracy to which they are submitted is far more rigorous than that which the peoples of the oldest democracies are even today undergoing.

England, France, Holland, Canada, Australia — these countries have never elected any candidate at large. Churchill was always and he still is the elected representative of his parliamentary district. So is Nehru in India, Abdul Rahman in Malaya, U Nu in Burma.

Before 1935, we never had any national election in this country. But our 1935 constitution abolished senatorial districts and by the 1940 amendments the nation was made to choose its senators at large and the people were burdened with an almighty, over centralized national government. Thus was the political machine enshrined and the will of the people made its slave instead of its master. A bill of rights protected the citizen's inalienable prerogatives, democracy was proclaimed — but everything else was done to make it as difficult as possible for the people to prove themselves equal to that democracy.

It is against this backdrop of handicaps, pressures and obstacles — that we can say that the showing of our people has been magnificent. They have proved themselves more mature than many nations around them by their performance in a test of maturity to which all circumstances considered no other nation in the world has ever been submitted. Assuming the absence of frauds, the returns show that at least 1,700,000 have voted for national candidates without machines, inspectors or lavish funds. They constitute almost a third of the voting electorate. Add to this the electors who voted freely for established party candidates and you will find that at least half of our electorate vote independently and with deliberation. This is more than can be said for some countries of Asia. This is more than can be said for some party-lining sections of the United States. A South American diplomat accredited to Tokyo told me recently that the showing of the Grand Alliance is of no precedence in Latin American countries. Indeed, I think we can claim as one of the achievements of our movement that it made concrete for the world to see the number of our independent electors and demonstrated beyond doubt our capacity for freedom.

Why do I say all of this here before homecoming Ateneo Alumni?

Because in the face of these repressive forces in our constitutional system, there have been liberating counter-forces in our society that have facilitated this magnificent showing of our people. There is the vigilant press. There are the militant civic organizations. There are the public school teachers. And here with us are the uncompromising men who through years of skepticism fought for the preservation of true liberal education, who insisted on teaching the universal and philosophical bases of freedom, on linking authority with God and on giving liberty such a solid value that it became worth dying for.

For 100 years, these men of Loyola — Filipinos, Americans and Spaniards — have woven into the fabric of our society the resistant strands of truth, wisdom and heroism from the same spool called the *ratio studiorum* with which they have thus fortified the pattern of other societies. By this consistent effort, the Ateneo in its first century assumed a unique role in the development of our nationhood.

**Raul S. Manglapus**                                                    **16**

# Faith in the Filipino

When the country needed national heroes, the Ateneo gave her the greatest of all. When she needed revolutionary generals, she gave her some. When she needed statesmen, trade unionists and men who could show others how to die for their country — she gave her many more. Now, in this her 100th year, what else is it that the Country can ask of the Ateneo which has given her so much?

When Father Cuevas brought back Jesuit education to the Philippines in 1859 it was to educate Filipinos not just for themselves but for their countrymen and for their God. Today, there are millions of our people living in barrios under the same conditions of poverty and destitution under which their ancestors lived when Father Cuevas arrived, nay, when the first Jesuits landed here 400 years ago. Our country has progressed but this progress has barely touched these orphans of our democracy. It is the challenge to the Ateneo that her sons should now be equipped, and more important, be inspired to turn their faces to this problem. This means a reduction to the first ends of the Ateneo. This means an intensification of that emotion which the Ateneo has ever generated — the love of country, the love of one's culture, one's land, and one's people.

Long before love of country was made a partisan political issue, we know that it was a primary counsel at the Ateneo which was followed in many forms. I remember that in 1940, when I was in the first year of law, our late beloved Father Joseph Mulry asked me to take advantage of our contact with President Quezon to suggest to him one of his pet projects — the establishment in the University of the Philippines of a college dedicated exclusively to research and study on Filipino culture so that this might serve as a nerve center for the reawakening of our people to their greatness as a nation. I went to see the President about it. He approved the idea and assigned it to one of his cabinet men for study but the war prevented its implementation.

We have had many Joseph Mulries as well as Joaquin Vilallongas at the Ateneo — Americans and Spaniards who successfully taught us to love the Philippines because they learned to love her first themselves. More and more, in the inevitable evolution of our nationhood, the Filipino Jesuits are taking up this work. And today, even if I am not a jubilarian, I feel a superior reason for joy because my own classmate of eleven years at the Ateneo is now her first Filipino rector.

Gentlemen of the Ateneo, only God knows whether in this generation, an Atenean shall ever lead this republic — whether Lacson. Padilla, Manahan, Osmena, Pelaez, Rodrigo or Recto will ever be President. But as long as we have Fritz Aranetas, aided for some time yet, we hope, by Mulries and Vilallongas, turning out lovers of their country, haters of compromise and challengers of despots — we need never worry about who is President. The collective impact of

Ateneans will always be there, tipping the balance in favor of progress, of truth, of faith and freedom.

-----

# III. The Church And Nationalism

**(Speech delivered at the Pax Romana Internatinal Conference, Manila, January 10, 1960)**

The terms of the subject assigned to me for development this afternoon are susceptible of widely divergent interpretations. Now one of the worst near-tragedies of recent times is that of the man who was put on trial for murder for having confessed to shooting George Bernard Shaw. The trial was finally stopped after the judge had ascertained the culprit's insistent clarificatory statement that George Bernard Shaw was the name of his neighbors dog whom he had caught eating the vegetables in his backyard garden.

I have no wish to be the victim of a similar tragedy, no matter how happily aborted. Permit me, therefore, to ensure that we shall be thinking if not alike, at least of the same things, and begin with a few definitions.

A nation is a substantially large group of people with common culture, customs, aspirations and racial characteristics. When to this is added a common government and a fixed territorial position, then we have a state — or more specifically, a national state. A state may embrace several nations. And a nation may be found populating several states.

Nationalism is love of nation, the promotion of the interesrs of one nation, the employment of this love among the people, among the nationals in order to propel the progress of the nation. In the context of world developments today, the termination as the object of this emotion of love may mean either of these possibilities — the nation as a cultural unit, the nation as a cultural and governmental unit or national state — or the nation as a state embracing several cultural units. The nationalism of the cultural unit within a state is usually directed by a cultural minority against engulfment either by a cultural majority or by an alliance of other cultural minorities. The nations engulfed by Soviet Russia on her western borders have the emotion of nationalism to resort to in their struggle to maintain their cultural identity and eventually to recover the identity of their national states.

But historical evolution, force, convenience, colonialism has compelled nationalism of this kind in most instances to give way and acceptance to the formation of states which are now called simply nations, embracing one or many groups of people which could by themselves have otherwise constituted nations in the larger and original sense. Thus is India today one state or one nation although she is really several nations brought together by many forces not the least of which was British power both as a coercive unifying force and in its negative role as provoker of the resistance which finally united the people of that sub-continent. Thus is the Philippines today. Although we could have instead several little sultanates for the Ilocanos, the Pampangos, the Tagalogs, the Cebuanos, the Boholanos, the Bicolanos, tlie Warays and the Ilongos.

Indeed, these latent nationalisms still persist today even if mostly in partisan exaggerations. Those of us who have at one time or other complained about oppression in the hands of the Ilocano nation, or the "Republic of Batangas", or if you will, of the "Republic of Bohol will find some consolation in the fact that even in solid, old Britain, there are "rumblings'* of revolt of the English majority against the "dominant association of Scots, Welsh, Irish. Cornishmen and Channel Islanders who are now running the British Government. Three months ago, the staid London "Economist" lamented in an editorial that English nationalism, inspite of this unbearable situation, has been quite dormant. The editorial hinted that it would like to see signs come up like "Quit England — Scots go Home as a manifestation of an awakened English nationalism. But this of course would mean booting out Prime Minister MacMillan liimself and sending him taking the high road home to Scotland!

All this illustrates some of the realities of nationhood development. If we can jest about the Ilocano nation today, and if the British, instead of fighting bloody tribal battles over it. can write tongue-in-cheek editorials about English nationalism, it is because wider nationalisms, the Philippine and the British, have each come to supplant peacefully and by force Ilocano and English nationalisms as political forms for participation in international intercourse and as instruments for the pursuance of certain destinies.

There is a certain artificiality in the development of modem nations which cannot escape us whether in the Oriental variety, represented by the Indian and Philippine experience, or the Occidental, illustrated by Britain. Historical accidents or incidents, such as the decision by the Spaniards not to take on Borneo or Celebes and by the stroke excluding them from the future Filipino nation — would seem to make of nation building a purely accidental series of events and not a guided process. This would lead us to have doubts about claims to "national destiny" and Divine design on the part of some nations, not excluding the Philippines. And yet faith and history teach us differently.

Nationalism — the driving urge of a people towards a common

destiny — may be traced back to the Jews. We know from our faith that they were a chosen nation — and to those who were not believers, the Jews proclaimed their destiny with pride. It was Cod, using Moses as His instrument, who led them out of their Egyptian bondage, who parted the waves of the Red Sea so that they might come to their promised land. God used nationhood and fostered nationalism for His divine ends. And then having made use of one nation as His agent, He decided not to destroy nationalism but to enlarge it — to give not only the Jews but all other nations a common destiny. He sent down His Son to become one of this fiercely nationalistic people and to surprise them by enjoining His apostles to go forth and "teach all nations" baptizing them in the name of the same Trinity and in the same Faith.

The nations that the apostles were supposed to seek out and persuade to this universal faith and destiny are now formed into nation states arrayed and impatient at the post. It look centuries before the modem national state could develop in the Western World — before loyalty to the feudal Lord or the city state could evolve into loyalty to a nation-state. In the East all this time, it was not nation building but empire building that preoccupied the emperors, the conquerors and the kings who spread the Mongol Empire from the Pacific to the Black Sea, who established the Turkish Empire in West Asia, the Mogul Empire in India, the Chinese Empire, and the loose empires of Shri Vishaya and Madjapahit in the Malay Archipelago.

It is not the slow and gradual development of Western nation states that draws our attention irresistibly today. It is the quick, dramatic, often violent eruption into Asian and African states of territories which barely ten years ago were governed by the West.

What role has the Church founded by Christ played in the molding of those new nationalisms? What role can she play in the shaping of their present and future direction?

It is the paradox of the times that the seemingly anti-Western nationalisms of Asia and Africa have been led by intellectuals inspired by Western ideas of constitutional democracy. Now these Western institutions were built on the basic Christian concepts of a social order, of the natural law that prescribed inalienable rights for man, of government authority coming from the governed, though ultimately from God.

Ideas of freedom it has been said need not be imported by a people. It is home grown everywhere in the hearts of men. Before these Western ideas were absorbed by Asian intellectuals, before Europe conquered the Orient, there were free communities all over Asia and words denoting freedom were found in every Asian language. But the art of constitutional democracy, which is the vehicle of Asian nationalism today, had to be learned through experience, through education and through the adoption of basic and guiding principles. Thus although we Filipinos have the Tagalog word "kalayaan" which means exactly freedom, we have no other word but the Spanish, and ultimately Greek, democracia to describe our constitutional system.

The avowed and burning objective of Asian nationalism today is the lifting of Asia's millions to a level of life worthy of the dignity of man. Mark that it is dignity and not merely equality that is sought after. Equality is inadequate because this shibboleth has not satisfied the masses who have indeed found equality with political independence — but equality in poverty and destitution. Dignity is better. It embraces legal equality and something more — the enjoyment of the fruits of the earth to an extent that will enable the citizen to keep his human dignity, to rise above the level of the irrational beast or the bare vegetative existence of the plant.

But why should man have dignity? Why is he better that the beast, the rock and the plant?

Four centuries ago, the Filipino learned why. He found the ready reason in the questions and answers of a little booklet called the "Caton Cristiano". This booklet was in later years to be much maligned as an instrument of a backward system of education that "brutalized rather than humanized the Filipino". The maligners would have preferred that he had been given a guide to better agriculture or a primer on parliamentary procedure. True, the Caton did not teach the Filipino the details of representative democracy. But it did teach him other important things — like the basis for the dignity of man which is the beginning of democracy. One of its questions asked "What Is Man?" and the answer said "Man is a creature made to the Image and likeness of Cod".

I doubt whether any other idea could have shocked the Filipino more quickly into a realization of his true worth as a man. He who had worshipped the trees, the sun, the sky. the spirits — to all of which he felt himself an inferior being, before whose Law, or perhaps more accurately. before whose caprices he was a helpless and absolute subject, gods that depressed rather than elevated his soul — this man suddenly found himself a creature in the image of His Creator, a participant in the likeness of an almighty but merciful God. What move compelling reason for seeking relief from subhuman existence, for driving towards a just share in the fruits of the earth?

Is it any wonder that fully fifty years before the fruition of other Asian nationalisms, Filipino intellectuals succeeded in persuading their people to a successful national revolution? The common man followed the intellectual because he knew, he had already been taught in its simplest but most impressive terms what the intellectual had elaborated for himself in the cultural centers of Manila and Madrid but had earlier learned from the same source — the Caton Cristiano.

# Faith in the Filipino

Man was made in the likeness of a Cod that asked of man to suffer and to work for his liberty. "To suffer, to work! What God is that?" asks Simoun in Rizal's Filibusterismo. Rizal answers the questions himself through Padre Florentino:

"It is the God of liberty, Senor Simoun, who obliges us to love it, by making the yoke heavy for us — a God of mercy, of equity, who while He chastises us, betters us and only grant prosperity to him who has merited it through his efforts, x x x.
"I do not mean to say that our liberty will be secured at the sword's point, x x x but that we must secure it by making ourselves worthy of it. by exalting the intelligence and the dignity of the individual, by loving justice, right and greatness, "even to the extent of dying for than, x x x"

This Christian concept of the dignity of man. whether in its original Catholic form, whether interpreted by the Catholic, the Anglican, the Presbyterian missionary, whether incorporated consciously or unconsciously in the writings of secular political scientists, found its way to the minds of intellectuals everywhere in Asia. It thus provided the basic philosophy for revolution not only against Western domination but also against indigenous absolutism such as the revolt against the Caliphate in Turkey and that against the Chinese monarchy lead by the Christian Sun Yat Sen.

But the most interesting study on the question of Christianity and Nationalism is to be made right here in this country. This is so because of the most thorough Christianization of our people in contrast to the rest of Asia. It was not the Philippines that the British historian Christopher Dawson was thinking of when he wrote:

"Western colonialism and Christian missionary action are two distinct forces, even though they are interrelated, and the former achieved its greatest success only when it had disassociated itself and completely from the latter, as the Dutch and the English East India companies both did in their palmy days. It is well-known that the Dutch retained their trade with Japan only by disassociating themselves entirely from Christianity, but it is even more significant that in Ceylon they took deliberate measures for the restoration of Buddhist Monasteries by importing reformers from Arakan in 1684 in order to weaken the existing native Catholicism. "In the same way, in India, the East India Company, far from acting as an agent of Christian propaganda, originally prohibited any missionary from entering the country and contributed to the maintenance of Hindu temples and the celebration of religious festivals like the great Jaganath pilgrimage of Purl*

*(Christopher Dawson, Christianity and

**Raul S. Manglapus**                                                          22

# Faith in the Filipino

*christian Culture, The Tablet (London))*

Not so, my friends, with Spain. While Britain and Holland came to Asia simply to trade, Spanish colonial policy was somewhat more elaborate. The Spaniards came for three things: God, Cold and Glory. Pursuing the same vigorous missionary action that transformed South American culture and civilization, the Spaniards succeeded in making Catholicism a truly Filipino religion, a task to which the political structure which they erected on these islands was both an advantage and a hindrance. The system by which municipal authority was given to the Spanish parish priest naturally discouraged vocations to the priesthood among Filipinos who were not to lie vested with governmental authority. We may go so far as to say that for this reason, the Spaniards themselves, while sincere in their desire to Christianize every Filipino, failed at least openly to encourage too many Filipino vocations. They thus were making their task of Christianization harder for themselves since, unlike the religion of Islam, Catholicism requires ordained ministers to spread its word and perform its sacramental functions.

In spite of this, Spain succeeded in performing in this country the universal mission of Christianity — that of making itself incarnate in every culture of the world. While in many places of Asia, Christianity remain a foreign faith, here it has become our own, has enriched our earlier culture without destroying it and permeated every aspect of our daily lives.

The permeation has been so complete that even the religious architectural art introduced by the Spaniards became distinctly Filipino. Just as the author Pari Relenten has established that the churches in Latin America are not just Spanish baroque but Latin American baroque*

*(Pari Relenten, Baroque and Rococo In Latin America.IN.Y: The Macmillan Company, 1951)*

so have a group of young artists recently established that the churches in Northern Luzon are not just Spanish but Ilocano baroque — born of local genius and fashioned with local materials, a distinctive style influenced but not entirely derived from the European form.*

*(Benito Legarda y Fernandez, Colonial Churches of Ilocos, Philippine Studies, Vol. VIII, No.1)*

National attitudes towards truth and goodness, towards law, towards justice, towards womanhood became Christian Filipino attitudes distinct from these in our geographical milieu. I might illustrate this by repeating, with your permission, a story which I told after

**Raul S. Manglapus**                                          23

returning home in 1956 from addressing the Asian Conference of Junior Chamber International in Singapore:

"Just two weeks ago at Singapore, I was approached by a distinguished Indian lady resident of that city, after I had delivered a speech on Asian emancipation. She said smilingly hut earnestly, 'You men are always talking of Asian emancipation. What about getting started on the emancipation of Asian women?'

"It was a crowded reception and I was shoved away from her before I was able to make a serious answer. But I was prepared to answer that it did not occur to me to mention the subject in my speech because the emancipation of women is something that we have taken for granted in this country for a long, long time. For the distinguished lady was referring not so much to the enfranchising of women — which of (nurse we have had here since 1936 — hut the rescuing of women from the category of chattel and their enshrining in their proper pedestal in the home. That. I believe, is something we have had here for centuries, inspired by the tenets of our Christian Faith which teaches that the women of the earth are to be honored, for they are so worthy of such honor that one of them even became the Mother of God."*

*(Raul S Manglapus. Freedom. Nationhood and Culture, pp. 181-182)*

This then is the manner that Catholicism has influenced the development of our nationhood. True, there were those Spaniards and overzealous hispanophiles who believed tliat the Filipino had first to be hispanicized or at least Europeanized before he was to be Christianized, a notion that has been repudiated with finality by Rome in the rather belated restoration of die practice of adopting Asian non-religious rites into Catholic services. But in all, the Catholic effort resulted as early as the middle of the nineteenth century in a sense of distinctness and oneness among our people which in the end enabled the intellectuals of that period to make use of the diffused spirit of reform which had manifested itself in scattered rebellions of former periods in one national movement which was finally successful.

This national movement was anti-clerical, that is, hostile to the Spanish clergy. This had to be since the Spanish cleric was himself a government functionary. Thus the propaganda of the revolution, following the new established pattern of war propaganda, had, for maximum effectiveness, to emphasize his human faults, of which there must have been, in fact, many, and de-emphasize his virtues, of which there were more. But the irrefutable proof that Philippine nationalism is Catholic precisely lies in this, that while the revolution against Spain was hostile to the Spanish clergy, it never developed to be truly anti-Catholic. The Aglipayan schism was partially successful only in the region of which the founder himself was native. And the Malolos Constitution by only one vote missed becoming the charter of a republic in which the Catholic Church and the State were united, a situation which even the most devout Catholic would not want to bring about today.

The reason for all this was of course simply that Catholicism had ceased to be just the religion of the state. It had become the religion of the people.

This Church that has provided the raison d'etre for sound nationalisms in the Western and Eastern world is now charged with being incapable of supplying the answer to their current demands and aspirations. The nations, old and new, want higher standards for every one, a bigger share of the goods that are made of the fruits of the earth. Asian communists have fashioned an even snappier charge— that the Church offers nothing but "pie in the sky when you die". We are told that the colonial mind is perpetuated by priests who tell the faithful to "suffer everything on earth to get a higher place in heaven".

That Christianity is out to save souls is true. It is truer to say that it is out to save men, that Christian salvation does not come as a reward after death but begins right here on earth and heaven is its final fulfillment. It is the mission of the Christian church to infuse itself in all branches of the human society, to transform it and direct it towards its eternal destiny. The Church has no detailed economic plan for the up-liftment of specific human communities. But it does offer principles and objectives which form the citizens' conscience and provide for the proper guidance of statement, lawmakers, civic leaders, trade unionists, business executives, and yes, economic planners.

"It is our will" said Pope Benedict XV, "that priests consider it as one of their duties to give as much of their life as possible to social science and social action, by study, observation and work ... Let no member of the clergy suppose that activity of this kind is something foreign to his priestly ministry because the field in which it is exercised is economic. It is precisely in this field that the eternal salvation of souls is imperilled"

In Quadragesimo Anno, Pope Pius XI laments, class war and exposes the evil of economic individualism. On the other hand he condemns the tyranny of unmitigated state socialism and proposes instead the principle of subsidiary function, that is, that the State has no right to control over activities which can be justly and effectively carried out by subordinate voluntary bodies, with the supreme goal always the common good of all.

In this and many other forms does the Church answer the legitimate demands of sound nationalism. And thus does it respond to the drive towards the enjoyment of God's gifts by all.

**Raul S. Manglapus**                                            **25**

But if nationalism can be sound, it is also inherently divisive. And so if its soundness is to be preserved, this divisiveness must be at least minimized, since, being inherent, it cannot be totally eliminated. The solution is to infuse into it the sobering strain of internationalism. The peoples of the world must be shown that it is possible to be nationalistic and still believe in international action. Even the communists while making use of nationalism for their ends will sing the "Internationale".

Indeed it is not only possible to be both nationalistic and internationalistic: today it has become impossible to achieve the necessary ends of nationalism without international cooperation.

But for international cooperation there must be peace. And the kind of world peace that is today required is not tlie Pax Romana imposed on a limited "known world by Roman legions nor a Pax Britannica brought about by the vigor of trading companies and the power of invincible navies. We do not seek, we are quite agreed. I hope, the soulless order of a Pax Sovietica. Nor, I am sure, are we anxious for a Pax Solum Americana. It is this Pax Romana, the spirit of peace, understanding and love that we seek, this spirit that is breathed in this meeting and its sister conference, where Christians have found a fresh understanding if not with at least of those of other faiths and of each other. This is the kind of peace in which true nationalism can thrive and seek its ends.

As for us Filipinos we have our own kind of internal peace to provide us with the setting for future achievement. It is the peace that came to the Filipino soul four hundred years ago, not by the so-called "discovery" of this archipelago by the Conquistador, but by the more genuine discovery of the truth of Christ by our people. All this, together with our own genius and other things such as our American constitutional experience, have given us what Toynbee calls an optimism that is found nowhere else in this part of God's world. It is thus, peaceful and optimistic that we now proceed to pursue the destiny in our Christian nationalism.

-----

# IV. The Message Of Western Europe

**(Speech delivered before the Manila Rotary Club, September 1, 1960)**

Some years ago, I was asked by the editors of a leading Manila paper to speak at a send-off dinner in honor of some students whom they had chosen for a free trip to Europe. The idea was for me to give them some words of advice on how best to profit from such a tour. It was a unique occasion and i accepted the invitation without much hesitation.

It was only when I sat down to put my advice to writing that it suddenly occurred to me that I was fundamentally unqualified for the task. I informed my hosts of my basic disability, but it was finally decided that there was no time for a change of speaker — and I went on to give the advice. I made sure, however, to anticipate charges of intellectual dishonesty by beginning with perhaps the most candid exordium that has ever been attempted. I said: "My friends, I have been asked this evening to give advice to young ladies and gentlemen on how best to profit from a trip to England. France, Italy and Spain. There is only one thing wrong with this picture. You see, I have never been to England, France, Italy or Spain."

I find myself in an even more difficult situation today. Indeed, it is not easy to give travel advice where both adviser and advised have not been anywhere near the place to be visited. But it is at least not lacking in verisimilitude and finds precedents in the most distinguished sources. For instance, the most immortal bit of advice to a departing traveller was that of Shakespeare's Polonius to his son Laertes, neither of whom had apparently ever been anywhere beyond the bounds of Hamlet's Denmark.

But now I am asked to report on a visit to Western Europe before recognized leaders of our affluent society, whose frequency of travel to that part of the world in response to the demands of their extensive interests are now limited only by the strange workings of the new multiple rate of foreign exchange. It is almost like trying to tell a German about Germany or a Japanese about Japan — or a Boholano about Bohol.

Sirs, when I received your cabled invitation I had just come from the British Parliament, the mother of national legislative bodies. There I had watched Prime Minister MacMillan in a robust and effective defense of his government's position in the matter of the shooting down of the RB47 aircraft which was alleged to have been based in England. What interested me at the time was not so much the merits of the case; certain facts surrounding it had then not yet come to light. What impressed me was the extra-ordinary vigor with which the Labor opposition, led by Mr. Hugh Gaitskell, sought to make much of the issue — a bit beyond the proportion which I thought it deserved.

I learned later why this was so. The British Labor Party once securely stood on such proper socialist planks as government control of production and socialization of services — things which make for a brilliant domestic platform. But since the conservatives returned to power, prosperity came to Britain. It came to the whole of Western Europe. The Laborites soon found that it is quite impossible to argue against prosperity. And so they have bad progressively to loosen their moorings from traditional socialism and must now seek instead to keep the party together by carrying the battle to the plane of foreign policy and national security.

When Berlin's spectacular Mayor Willy Brandt leads the West German Socialist Party in next year's elections against Adenauer and the Christian Democrats, he will not insist that socialism replace the free enterprise which has sent prosperity rolling on the autobahns. He will seek to show himself the better leader in the face of the Soviet threat, the better bargainer with the new friends of the West and perhaps the man with the better plans for the re-unification of the Fatherland. For nowhere in Western Europe is free enterprise prosperity so evident and so defiant of challenge as in the Federal German Republic. And nowhere is this defiance more dramatic than in Berlin itself, where by simply crossing a street one may go from the abundance, the optimism and the verve of the Western sector to the barrenness of the East Berlin shops and the drab, slogan-laden life which socialism in its most fundamental form has imposed upon a people.

The social democrats everywhere in Western Europe have begun to face this reality. To pursue their laudable and, we must add, necessary ends of increasing labor participation in management affairs, they have ceased to cry for government control and for the destruction of private enterprise. Instead they would fight within the framework of the free system. In Germany, this decision has borne fruit in the development of what is now called co-determination — a system by which labor is represented on "Supervisory Boards" in major industries. In Italy, this experiment has been tried successfully in the Olivetti factories.

But if labor leadership is intensely interested in such compromises of the socialist ideal, the workers themselves apparently are not. In Germany the workers worry much more about the problem of parking space. And everywhere in Europe, as one company director put it "the workers are not interested in the problems of management; they debate mostly on where to go for the summer in their new cars — whether to the French or the Italian Riviera".

Most of you have seen the Volkswagens, the Dauphines the Fiats and the Seats of the Western European worker rolling merrily indeed to that vacation at the Riviera, the Costa Brava, the Alps. You have seen their factories when the problem is how to keep up with the demand and where the lament is not that they have to turn away many job applicants but that they can not get enough to apply. Whence come such bursting economies? Indeed tribute is to be paid to the thoroughness of the German, the resourcefulness of the British, the cleverness of the French, the daring of the Italian. These do not suffice to explain the industrial prosperity of Western Europe. And it is no disparagement of these national qualities to seek the supplementary reasons for this phenomenon.

When World War II broke out Western Europe was in an advanced stage of industrial development. So, in fact, were some parts of Eastern Europe. Rostow, explaining his theory of stages of economic growth, states that when the communists took over in Russia in 1917, they inherited an economy which had already "taken off". He defines economic take-off as that short stage of development concentrated within two or three decades, in which the economy and the society of which it is part transform themselves so that economic growth becomes more or less automatic.

The war did not cause a paralyzation of industry. It caused an adjustment of production which in most cases invigorated rather than hampered industrial development. Certain industrial centers were heavily damaged but on the whole, the industrial complexes of Western Europe survived intact on both sides. For instance in August, 1943, the RAF bombed the city of Hamburg so devastatingly that Hitler was heard for the only known time during the war to say that it might be necessary to sue for peace. A third of the city was levelled to the ground, but the industrial plants around the edge and the submarine pens on the harbor were hardly damaged. The grave social dislocation at the end of the war aggravated the problems of resumption of production and employment — but there was enough capital resource with which to proceed, following Rostow's concept, to new stages of growth.

It was to these ready, receptive and eager economies that the Marshall plan then brought to bear its massive, intelligent and efficient aid. Joined to the genius of each receiver nation and the irrepressible propulsion of private enterprise, there was only one result that the plan could bring about — success.

Why do I trouble to analyze the economic greatness of Western Europe? Because it is dazzling and cannot escape attention and while some Filipinos viewing it might take heart from it, altogether too many might find in it reason for despair. Without careful analysis, it is too easy, as I am afraid some have already done, to explain our inability to come anywhere near it in toms of sheer native ineptitude. No one in Western Europe, certainly not the German who has seen the folly of the cult of superman, will claim his country's economic stability as coming from sheer native aptitude.

It is also all too easy to blame the lack of massive aid for economic insufficiency. We regret that there was never any serious talk of a Marshall plan for Asia. But bow much of that massive aid could our Asian economies have absorbed efficiently in the early post-war years?

# Faith in the Filipino

It is, alas, even easier to talk of the economic short-cut. Ignoring the large scale discreditation of orthodox socialism in Western Europe, there are a few who would suggest that European prosperity could be ours — if we took the swifter, more efficient socialist road — the very road that Western Europe has shunned.

Careful analysis can lead to saner attitudes. There is every indication not only that Western European prosperity is not beyond our reach — but that we may well be at least in the beginning of the road to its attainment. One Filipino economic historian has categorically stated that (again to pursue the Rostow concept) we are already on the take-off stage.

If we have readied this stage, it is due to a maturization and expansion of the middle class created in this country by mercantile operations in tlie nineteenth century which provided the leadership for the first successful national revolution in colonial Asia in 1896. in this century this class was widened by universal education, and the common application of constitutional democracy. In the whole of Asia, only Japan may lay claim to have reached and passed this stage. And we possess, outside of Japan, the widest enterpreneurial and technological base. It is a tribute to our people's genius that we have reached all this inspite of suffering the gravest damage in this part of the world during the war — and in spite of travesties on our democracy by the professional politician.

If we are indeed on the right road — how much shall we progress from here? What shall be our pace? Shall we allow others around us to pass us by our own indecision, by our own pessimism, by our own fears?

If it is evident that it is private enterprise that has been the propelling force in our drive to economic maturity, how much are we going to allow it now to continue and to accelerate this propulsion? Or, for the sake of self-perpetuation in political power, is our present leadership going to deny us what, alas, no past leadership ever came to grant us, the liquidation of those giant institutions, absorbers of political patronage, once excused as stimulators now stiflers of private initiative.

There is, for instance, the business of banking. No one will dispute the readiness of private Filipino enterprise to assume increased participation in banking operations in this country. Is it not time to strike down one of the greatest obstacle to this increase — that sprawling monster called the Philippine National Bank? The PNB has had its days pioneering, and in certain sections of the country, such trail-blazing activities may still be required.

But is there any reason why its central activities should be allowed to continue? Is there any reason why, when private enterprise is ready for so much more, it should continue to carry on almost half of the banking business in the country? Is there any reason why it should continue to be the sole depository of treasury funds, depriving our private banks of this rich source of capital support which their counterparts elsewhere, particularly in the United States, have long enjoyed?

No, reason there is none. But there are excuses. There is one which goes as follows: no one can afford to buy the PNB. It will cost too much. It will cost too much because there are so many accounts that swell its value — mostly political accounts — loans given out by direction of several administrations — loans that were never meant to be collected.

The government has made enough out of the PNB. And the PNB was never meant to make money for the government. It was meant to pioneer. If in order to bring down its book value to the reach of private enterprise, it must write off these political accounts, I say write them off. Write them off now, because they will never diminish but instead continue to increase with not a prospect of payment. Write them off now because it is now that private enterprise requires this boost.

As with banking so with insurance. Our insurers have shown the same capacity and vigor that our bankers have displayed. There is no reason — and no excuse — why the insuring of government employees should not be entrusted to private insurance companies.

Ah, but if there is no reason and no excuse, there are motives. These institutions are not just instruments of public financing. They are instruments of power. They are clubs over the heads of planters, millers, manufacturers, importers, citizens of every class, clubs to be wielded at the supreme moment when election funds must be had with which to buy the votes of the people.

So many eloquent voices are raised today against personal corruption in the government, voices from the opposition, voices within the administration and the party in power itself. Where is the voice that will call for an end to the institutional extortion that is perpetrated upon the people at every election time through the medium of government financing institutions?

The integrity and efficiency of anyone connected with these establishments are not at issue. We all deeply admire many such past and present officers. What is under indictment is the party in power and other parties in power before it. A law, thank God, has been passed to prevent and prosecute personal dishonesty in official positions. Will anyone in Congress — from any party — now submit a bill to prevent and prosecute this group malfeasance, this collective dishonesty of which no party that has ever been in power may be absolved? Indeed, this gross and unsubtie coercion, unique in representative governments today, has happened before. And it is fast becoming a science applied with deathly regularity every two years. Its victims are many freedoms — the freedom of political action, the freedom of choice, the freedom of private enterprise, the freedom of speech.

If our economy is to grow, it must be released from the suffocating chambers within which government interference has kept it prisoner and allowed to breathe and expand in the free air of private enterprise. There is an urgency to this matter which we who live in tlie buzzing industrial complex around Manila may not realize. Millions of our multiplying countrymen have not been touched by all this activity. I suggest we avoid contenting ourselves with our own personal successes. I suggest we think with the Filipino resident of a British colony who said to me last month: "We Filipinos will be great when we get to be like the British. The British are great because they feel a personal diminution whenever they see a fellow Britisher living in poverty."

The next stages of growth are within our reach. But now that we are on our way, it is time to provide for safeguards so that the material progress which we pursue may not one day outstrip our cultural and spiritual development. In Berlin, I attended the Congress for Cultural Freedom. a meaningful exchange of views in the middle of Communist territory between the articulate intellectuals of the free world. There the frustrations of those who live in the affluent societies of mass consumption were given full expression. Possessing all the cars, the houses, the TV sets, the refrigerators, the radios that they can use, some cynical leaders of Western thought went so far as to suggest that all these things having produced nothing but empty, purposeless lives and high rates of suicide, perhaps Asian societies should not be encouraged to pursue their possession.

Those who propose this extreme view are men who in their personal lives have felt the hollow impact of the outstripping of spiritual growth by material expansion. This need not be true for everyone not for every society. When I arrived last week a friend who had been to Germany said to me: "So you have seen West Germany. Didn't you get the feeling that you were seeing one huge, efficient, cold IBM machine?" This was a man who had spent a few days in that country visiting the magnificent factories and the neat, modem, superb reconstruction in big cities linked together by the network of incredible autobahns.

He had not been to any of the gay beer-halls in Munich, had not heard a single Bavarian band, had not experienced the deep devotion of the Oberammergau Passion Play, had not listened to a Cardinal rally his faithful in Berlin, had not watched German drama, had not read that in that country are currently being exerted the most determined efforts of the two splintered halves of Christianity to find common ground for unity — all those things by which the Germans are striving mightily so that the German soul does not die but rather gives meaning to German prosperity.

We too have a soul that need not die when we shall have achieved our material millenium. It is a great soul, a hybrid soul to be sure, as is the British. But then, as the British Ambassador here has said with just and pardonable pride, it is those civilizations of hybrid origins that have achieved a real greatness. It is tlie appointed task for you who are privileged to be laying the material foundations for that greatness to see to it that as our pride in our economic achievements increase, so does our pride in our spirit, in our culture, in our race.

That pride need not be vain and baseless. In one of the great European capitals I was taken to see a hall of fame. There, my distinguished guide pointed out, is a poet, here a linguist, this one a novelist, that a physician, lie a sculptor, this a dramatist, now a historian, this a man who inspired our revolution, and that a man who died for this country.

We have no wonderful halls of fame such as this, I regretfully admitted to my host. But then, I said, it is perhaps because with one statue we could have all that we find here. There was one Filipino who was all this — poet, novelist, sculptor, biologist, physician, dramatist, linguist, historian — who inspired our revolution and who died for his country. His name was Jose Rizal.

Yours must be a great race, said my host. There is no equal figure in the history of Europe.

That, indeed, was a compliment. We might also wish to take it as the message of Europe to us — greatness is in all men and in all races — it is within the reach of anyone nation that seeks it and it will endure as long as it is faithful to that nation's spirit.

-----

# V. Jazz, Culture And Politics

**(Speech delievered at the Jazz Concert, De La Salle College, Manila, September 12, 1960.)**

You are probably wondering what a frustrated politician like me is doing at this |azz concert.

Frustrated politicians find renewed inspiration in jazz. We are politicians in a democratic order and there is no more successful democratic operation than that of a good jazz group. To put it in more contemporary terms — there is more successful democracy in the republic of the combo than in the republic of Congo.

# Faith in the Filipino

Why do I say that the combo is a republic and an eminently successful one?

What is a democratic republic but a conglomeration of people, each with his own designs, is own opinions, his own objectives, kept together only because, the principle of responsible liberty and thus somehow making a unified whole. That is what a combo is — a conglomeration of men, each with his own designs, instruments, ambitions, each going into his own wild, personalized improvisation — kept together only by one melodic theme but somehow making a harmonious whole.

You will therefore understand why men like me would go the extent of forming our own combo in order to make up for the political frustration which is in the very air that we breathe today.

There is an even more compelling reason for anyone interested in culture to be interested in jazz. My reference to the combo and the Congo was more than just a play on words. Jazz, as you know, is basically the Negro's art. It began as a folk art but is now a universal art form. If universality is the supreme achievement of all art forms, then we must hail jazz as having come into its artistic maturity. It has been embraced, embellished and given infinite new dimensions in Scandinavia, Australia, Brazil, Bangkok, Iceland, Tokyo and Rome.

The first literature on jazz that ever fell in my hands was a huge book written by the Frenchman Huges Panassie. It was entitled "Le Jazz Hot" and it was given to me before the war by a young Frenchman by the name of Jean Levy-Reldy who was for a time a student here at La Salle. The latest authoritative book on it is by Andre Hodeir who says that nothing is more reassuring to humanity than the universal diffusion of the message of jazz. Indeed, it has been alleged by American pundits that Americans may play good jazz but the French talk the best jazz in the world.

Whether this is true or not, the most stimulating developments in jazz today are going on in Western Europe. Jazz artists like Armstrong, Ellington, Gillespie and the late Sidney Bechet have been applauded through France, Germany, England, Holland, Scandinavia, in the same concert halls as Gieseking and Menuhin. To illustrate the universal European appeal of jazz: the latest jazz festival at Antilles, on the French Riviera, was reported to have been attended by combos from Communist satellite countries.

Even the restrained Englishman has succumbed. When I was in England last July as a guest of the British Council, a most efficient Council official said to me "Sir, we have prepared a rather tight schedule for you as you can see, but we did leave a few free evenings which you might wish to fill in with visits to British cultural spots of your choice". I said "what would you say if I wanted to look into the development of British jazz — would you think it a good idea?" She said I'd say it was a jolly good one. We must ring up Humphrey Littleton".

Humphrey Littleton is the leading exponent of British jazz. Unfortunately he was out in Liverpool somewhere. But his manager Peter Burman took us around the extremely crowded jazz dubs in London. There are progressive clubs which are called "modern" and Dixieland or traditional which are called "mainstream". The modernists are rather proud of their stock and one of them said to me about a Dixielander "There goes Peter Harrington -- he's mainstream. Pity, really. Nice chap, ottherwise, you know".

In all of these dubs, which are all dean, wliolesome ones where only ice cream and cokes are served, I announced myself for purposes of proper accreditation as an honorary member of the Jazz Society of the Philippines. I must ask Nelda Navarro here whatever has happened to that dub.

In one of these clubs, I met a most articulate and most charming young lady, Miss Pamela Bavin who is associate editor of the Canadian Jazz Magazine "Coda", a copy of which I have here with me tonight. It is an unpretentious but most satisfying publication. Let me read to you what one commentator in it says about Russ Wilsons view of jazz in the context of world economic and social development. It supports, I think, my outlook on the universality of jazz and of culture in general.

"Russ thinks jazz is a whole culture created from conditions existing during different eras & phases of social behaviour & economic development gotten as by-products out of the varied & quite different national cultures formed from religious & social needs and that now has become a separate universal culture out of, for & by the people . . . A CULTURE called JAZZ."*

*(CODA, The Canadian Jazz Magazine, June, 1960)

Indeed, we should keep in touch with jazz clubs all over the world. Jazz here should have a worthy magazine and a club that would correspond everywhere. There is so much of our jazz to be proud of, as is being demonstrated here this afternoon. Perhaps we should sponsor a tour of a Filipino combo in Europe.

Vic Perez and his progressives are a typical thing that we can be proud of. By the way, progressive jazz has been criticized as an attempt to dignify jazz by introducing classical strains in it. Dave Brubeck has been subjected to this sort of attack.

Actually we might speak in exactly opposite terms. It is jazz that has lately if not dignified at least given freshness and vitality to European dassical music — Schoenberg, Webern, Berg, Bartok. Ravel, Milhaud, Stravinsky have shown the salutary effect that jazz can have on classical music. Stravinsky for instance has shown this in his "Histoire du soldat", Ragtime pour onze instruments" and "Piano Rag Music"; Milhaud in his "La creation du monde" and Ravel in "L'enfant et les sortileges".

Although I am partial to Dixieland and mainstream — I appreciate and indulge in progressive anti Latin jazz and in that sort of in between called bop — so brilliantly interpreted by Nelda Navarro.

I congratulate tlie Chemical Engineering students of this college for this successful concert. And for those who may have been a bit shocked that this distinguished Catholic institution should now be the situs for this concert — I might mention a pertinent bit of contemporary ecclesiastical history. In the spirit of the ecumenical movement, the church encourages the growth of local rites and the use of local customs and languages. In some parts of Africa, the Mass has been said to the rhythm of that Negro folk art which we know by the name of Jazz. In a recent TV jazz show in the United States the outstanding performers were a group of Franciscan brothers. I am not suggesting that Brother Denis should take to the saxophone and organize the FSC combo. Although I think that would be an exciting idea. Imagine the snappy names they could call themselves, such as "Denis' Menaces".

But perhaps it might be a good idea to include jazz contests as an NCAA activity and improve the students' culture as well as their physique.

I have said enough — and after hearing me thus far you must be fully agreed that jazz is better played than talked.

Let's play it.

-----

# VI. Youth - A Return To Leadership

**(Speech delivered al the Award Ceremony of the Junior Chamber of Commerce for the Ten Outstanding Young Men (TOYM), Luneta. Manila. October 2, 1960.)**

We are here to honor by this ceremony ten outstanding young Filipinos. Something else is here outstanding besides these ten young men. It is this ceremony itself. It stands out because it is unusual, because it has taken the special efforts of a distinguished publication and of a militant civic organization to lift the achievements of these youths from the context of our national life in order that they might be held up for the nation to see, to appreciate and to reward.

There was a time in our history when such special efforts were not required, when the achievements of youth needed no such particular proclamation. It was a time of change, of awakening, of revolution — and achievements by youth were more commonplace than unusual.

Let me take you back to January 23, 1899. In Malolos it is the day of the inauguration of the First President of the Philippines. His name is Emilio Aguinaldo. His age is 29.

The men around him are not much older: Mabini is 34, Calderon, 30, Lukban, 31, Albert, 32. His republic is the frail flower of the revolution which was watered by the blood of men like Bonifacio, who led the Katipunan at 29, Antonio Luna, who was a general at 29, Emilio Jacinto, who was killed at 23.

In Spain itself, Lopez Jaena had begun to sow the seeds of that revolution at 20; and there had followed Marcelo del Pilar at 32, Panganiban at 32. Ponce at 25.

Let us follow Aguinaldo as he vainly seeks to keep his republic alive. In Palanan, in March of 1901, he is surrounded and captured. But before this, tliere is a general who gives his life for his President — Gregono del Pilar. He is 24.

The republic is defeated and a new effort at independence begins. Osmena is Speaker of the House at 29. Quezon is Commissioner in Washington at 32. Laurel is Secretary of the Interior at 32. Roxas is Speaker at 29.

These were our outstanding young men in the days of conflict, of struggle, of revolution. To prove their excellence there was little need for ceremony such as this which we hold here. Their achievements required little effort to proclaim, because leadership was theirs, and they gave rise to ceremony — ceremony did not give rise to them.

Why is this not so today? Has our nation grown so old before its time? Have we so quickly, so prematurely outgrown the spirit of change, of reform, indeed of revolution? What has brought us to this, that we must search in the haystack for youthful achievements and organize occasions for their recognition?

I hope that we have not begun to think that the period of revolution is over for us. We do not need a revolutionary war. We do need revolutionary ideas — ideas by which to keep ourselves from static complacency, by which to bound forward, unfettered by the chains of the status quo.

I hope that we have not begun to think of freedom as in itself an all-satisfying end. That it cannot be. Democracy is an atmosphere and in its free air a nation may grow in its body and in its spirit. But the nation will not grow simply because it is democratic. It will grow if its citizens, taking advantage of this freedom, will ceaselessly conceive of new ideas, plan them, implement them so that the people may push forward in their march to a better life.

**Raul S. Manglapus**                                    **37**

# Faith in the Filipino

We cannot end the search for the revolutionary idea. We must carry it on among the young, for when one is young, it is then that one is impatient for change. The First Christian Revolutionary was 12 when He hinted about His revolution. He was 30 when He began it. And He was 33 when He died for it The spirit of His revolution has never died.

One wonders whether our revolutionary spirit has died all too soon, and whether, it this is so, it is because our young men have forfeited the leadership in the continuing revolution. What are the Filipinos of the age of Aguinaldo in Malolos, of del Pilar in Palanan, of Osmena in the Assembly — what are they doing while the tired old men squabble over the destinies of our country?

There is only one thing worse then that youth should surrender the leadership in the continuing democratic revolution. It is this — that having thus surrendered, they should yield the initiative to their fellow young men who have taken up the leadership in a new revolution that seeks to destroy human liberty.

Is this not what is happening m our country? How many of you young men standing before me today —bearing arms in the name of democracy — will match the ardor of your counterparts who seek to infiltrate your ranks, your classrooms, your campuses, your activities, your very lives in the service of a Godless revolution? How many of you would be ready to lay down your lives for freedom as they are willing to lay down theirs for slavery, even before the battle begins and even if it never begins?

I hope that the answer to that question is "all of us!" For it is the only way — the response of an equal determination — that this new revolution can be stopped. A revolutionary idea can only be stopped by another revolutionary idea, or, if you will, by the impact of several revolutionary ideas or revolutionary men.

Fortunately, we have such an impact to inspire us here today. In this gathering there are ten young men who are being tappet for recognition because by their work, by their genius and by their example they have made refreshing and propelling changes in many otherwise static aspects of our society. You have heard the great things for which they are cited. Surely we have here the hope that the initiative can be regained, that youth is returning to leadership and that our freedom may be all the more alive.

The rules of this contest have required that only those be considered who are between the ages of 21 and 35. It is thus that there is added significance in the choice of place for this ceremony today. For oil this hallowed ground, there is revered the memory of a Filipino who. if I might be colloquial, would have "just made" the contest. For when he was put to death for believing in liberty, he was 35.

I am certain that the spirit of Rizal, the most outstanding young man of the Philippines in 1896 — indeed, the most outstanding young man in the history of his nation and of his race, smiles upon us this morning. For it is no less than the return of that spirit that we here celebrate.

-----

# VII. A Time To Choose Goals

**(Speech delivered before the Cebu Rotary Club,
October 27, 1960.)**

I should like to begin by repeating a true story related to me the other day by Mr. Jim Becker, Manila chief of bureau for the Associated Press. It seems that last June an American friend of his was in Manila for a visit. After a couple of days of reading the newspapers, listening to the radio and meeting citizens of this gay republic, the visitor was moved to remark that there seemed to be a great deal of heated interest among the population in candidates for the coming elections. The visitor inquired incidentally when these elections were coming.

"In November" he was told.

"What?" he exclaimed incredulously "still five months away and already so much noise?"

"My dear fellow" Jim said pianissimo trying to break it to him as gently as possible "it isn't this November — it's November of next year!"

I am told that at that juncture rudimentary first aid had to be administered to the visitor.

Gentlemen, I think we can all agree that there is tragic truth in this comic story. There is tragedy that comes in many forms.

One is that, because we have elections every two years, there is hardly any breathing spell left for our people in between periods of political campaign.

Another is that since these elections are, because of the senatorial struggle, always national in character, they dominate the actions and motivations of both majority and minority politicians — and the public weal is forever subordinated to the necessity to win the elections that are with such fatal consistency always impending.

Still another is that since so many candidates must be nationally and not just locally elected, the people must ever be submitted to the blandishments of men seeking a national "build-up".

The most amusing tragedy is this — that since the two major parties are assured of perpetual existence by the inspector law, safe from successful challenge by any upstart young party, it has not been their concern to present concrete programs to the people — the "outs" have been quite content to push out the "ins" on the eternal issue of graft and corruption.

The result is that the electorate has been trained to vote on purely negative issues — only on what is wrong with the performance of one party and not on what is right with the program of another. Worse, since party platforms hardly differ, nothing wrong is thought of party-hopping. Hopping from one political party to another becomes as common as hopping from one cocktail party to another and the people rather cynically have begun to think of it as evidence of political astuteness, indeed of political maturity, rather than as a clever piece of political immorality. There is a unique and astounding by-product of this interesting process — from first sight of which the visitor needs more than just rudimentary first aid to recover — a phenomenon peculiarly Filipino -- the thirteenth wonder of the world — the "guest candidate"!

It has been seriously suggested in fact that we junk the entire tourism development program and concentrate instead on taking our tourists on guided tours of our political circuit. This would be cheaper and much more amusing for our visitors.

Since everyone assumes quite correctly that party platforms are all alike, political attention is then concentrated on party candidates. Personal leadership becomes the issue in local and national encounters and there is frantic scrambling and realigning even before the smoke of one battle has cleared.

Thus, you and I have lately been importuned with the persistent question "who are you for?" But nobody bothers to ask anybody "what are you for?"

I could make more noise today indeed if I started to tell you who I was for. But I thought the gentlemen of Cebu Rotary would rather like to know if I stood for anything at all these days. I thought you might find the idea a refreshing one. And so, I have taken the liberty of putting down my own favorite set of objectives in public issues. These things, gentlemen, I stand for today.

First, I have no wish to ignore the best known issue of the day — dishonesty and graft. What I reject is the idea that graft can be eliminated simply by a change of party or a change of men. Such a change can become necessary but can never be the absolute remedy. I hold, and for some time now I have been emphasizing this at every opportunity, that the holiest of men can be tempted with too much power and that our constitutional system has placed too much power in the national government.

This near absolute power manifests itself in many ways and it is no problem to pinpoint these manifestations. It is manifested in the minutely detailed power in Malacanang over the release and disposition of huge funds for public improvements, over the approval of the smallest loans in monstrous government lending institutions. It manifests itself in the legislative, in the all-embracing power of appropriation of national funds — funds extracted by the almighty power of taxation from barrios, from municipalities, from cities, from provinces that are left with the crumbs and that then must come to Manila to beg for what is rightfully theirs.

There are two key steps to the solution of this problem. One is the dispersal and redistribution of power, a process embodied in the term decentralization that word which strikes fear in the heart of the professional politician who lives on patronage and whose leadership depends on precarious ties with national officials. The other is the reduction of those giant government financing enterprises to limits required in pioneering fields. This process is feared by many kinds of people — the majority party fund raiser whose job is simple — lowering the boom on crop loan applicants before every election; the cheap ten-percenter who makes a dishonest living following up loan application; the twenty-four carat executive who makes a more honest living by demanding fifty percent!

I do not stand for dispersal of power and for striking down these government monsters only because I would thus like to see graft minimized. I stand for those things principally because of their positive consequences. I am for dispersal of power because this means strengthening our local institutions and revitalizing the initiative of our millions. I am for striking down government businesses because this means the unchaining of private enterprise — and I have seen unchained private enterprise producing solid prosperity for the great democracies of the world.

I stand for bolder and more imaginative programs within this our chosen framework of free initiative. And there is room for such boldness. Recently, someone thought of organizing a cigarette factory. He had the managerial ability but he had no capital. Government credit was tight — a loan or two were available but at a rate of "pabagsak" he could not afford. So he decided to stop looking for capital in Manila and to go to the people themselves.

He gathered a group of fanners in tlie Ilocos and explained his project. He showed how it would bring employment to their community and provide a market for their tobacco produce. But, lie said "I don't think we can do it because I have no capital." "We have capital right there" said one fanner, 'how much do we need?"    Our friend gave his figure. It was a big one but he was surprised that the farmers were not dismayed. One pledged five hundred pesos. Another a thousand. "At this rate," thought the organizer, "we'll never make it. But an old woman asked that she be given a minute to fetch her money from home. She came back with some savings which she had been hiding under her bed. The amount was P90.000!

We have heard of cooperative labor. Here Is new and more exciting project — cooperative capital. For of visible labor we have an excess. But we also have plenty of invisible capital, hidden in bamboo safes and under straw mattresses. I am for imaginative and forceful measures that will coax this wealth from its retirement and put it to work for our economy.

I am for a total campaign for capital. This means that where domestic capital is found insufficient — and in some fields of activity it has been found insufficient — we must open the door — not reluctantly, not half-heartedly but with gusto and with aggressive determination to lay down coherent and attractive terms for the entry of foreign capital. This means calling an end to irresponsible oratory that contradicts avowed policy and repels the most interested of investors. This means following in the footsteps of many young states of Asia and Africa which have outpaced our country in the race for foreign investment by their positive and intelligible policies and by their consistency of attitudes. I am for the abolition of those impediments, such as the capital gains tax, which discourage the transfer of capital from unproductive, static investments to productive enterprise.

I am for total decontrol, when, and only when, we are ready with the leak-free tariff wall with which to protect our young industries. In lieu of such a wall, I would favor preferential rates of foreign exchange to keep these industries from dying young in the battle of the free market.

I am for a few other things, one of which I may have time to mention today. I am for strengthening the civil service not by eloquently invoking constitutional safeguards but by admitting the possibility that these safeguards may not be enough and going about making up for their deficiency. I reiterate my proposal for the creation of an executive academy, perhaps under the aegis of the institute of Public Administration of the University of the Philippines, which would graduate men and women educated in the broad principles of public administration and each specialized in one of the many aspects of government — including the foreign service. I would then seek constitutional amendment so that these graduates would bold exclusive right to appointment to positions of responsibility in government bureaus, offices and departments up to and exclusive of cabinet category.

These are not impossible goals. They are not the dreams of an idealist.

Decentralization is a fact in England, in Germany, in Australia, in India, in Malaya, in the United States — all countries where power is dispersed, where men in office are least tempted and where the individual is permitted his initiative and self-respect.

# Faith in the Filipino

Unchained private enterprise is a fact in Western Europe, in the United States, in Australia, in Canada, where unprecedented prosperity is today providing more goods than ever for contented populations.

Vigorous policies of attraction are drawing millions of dollars in foreign capital into India, Pakistan, Vietnam, Malaya, Nigeria, Ghana, Australia — and even into the advanced economies of Western European nations.

Civil service and foreign service academies are a reality in Germany, Indonesia, Vietnam, England, India and some states of the United States.

I am told by some nervous friends that this is the time to choose sides, meaning to choose men to follow and support in the coming Presidential campaign. Choose sides, I am advised, and talk of platforms and programs later.

I disagree. I will not blindly follow anyone who comes and says "Elect me or reelect me — my election or reelection will solve everything," I will not follow such a man because I would immediately suspect him of a Messianic complex. But there would be nothing wrong with a Messiah if he had a program to offer. The true Messiah had such a program —such a solid one that it has worked for two thousand years.

I have said more than once that I favor a unified opposition. What I do not favor is unification with no binding principle save the desire to have specific men elected or to bring down the administration. Such a coalition would be ephemeral and could collapse quickly, even before the elections — as was the fate of last year's attempt.

I think it is time the Filipino people began to depend on concrete programs of government for their salvation. There is no guarantee that the search for new Quezons and Magsaysays will ever be fruitful. As the search is prolonged, millions of our countrymen await impatiently to be touched by the benefits of industrial democracy. In this context, I favor a union of men who can go to the people and tell them not only how good they are — but more especially how good their goals are and what they propose to do to achieve them. Such a union, I think, could last and I have every confidence that it would find support.

I have attempted to offer you today a few points in humble contribution to that set of objectives by which such men might be united. You may not agree with some or any of them. But I suggest to you that as leaders of your community it is your task to consider carefully the bases on which you are to pick the choices that are given you in those crucial hours of our democracy.

The first choice, I insist, is not tike choice of men. It is not even

**Raul S. Manglapus**                                                    **43**

the choice of parties. It is the choice of principles, of programs, of the roads to take towards economic, political and spiritual growth. Having made this choice, we may then use it to measure the worth of individual leadership. Only thus, it seems to me, can we hope to reach maturity as a nation of freemen.

-----

# VIII. Old Lessons For A New Future

**(Speech delivered at the Commonwealth Anniversary Dinner, Philippine Columbian Association, Manila. November 15, 1960.)**

There is someone in this audience to whom I made a solemn promise that my speech this evening would not linger in the past but would concentrate on the promise of the future. To him I must apologize in advance. For tonight I propose to linger quite a bit in that past before attempting to turn to that future.

I must add in explanation that I tried to fulfill my promise to the letter. But I found after I had sat down to write that I could not look forward with a clear vision without first looking behind.

There is a Tagalog saying which goes as follows: *"Ang hindi marunong lumingon sa pinanggalingan ay hindi darating sa pinaparoonan".* Our charming tagalista Mrs. Hickerson will confirm that this means that one who does not know bow to look back to his beginnings will never reach his destination. To paraphrase it, one can not properly choose his future course without knowing where he comes from; one cannot pretend to speak of change and redirection without understanding what there is to change and what points of departure there exist from which to redirect a forward movement.

George Santayana put it this way in his famous epigram: "They who cannot remember the past are condemned to repeat it".

In 1940, just a few steps from where we stand here tonight, I witnessed a debate on the subject of bicameralism vs. unicameralism sponsored by the Civil Liberties Union. It was held at the auditorium of the Ateneo where I was then a student, and it was broadcast to the whole nation. Two men carried on the discussion, one standing on the stage, speaking for the revival of the senate, the other in the right proscenium box, seeking the continuation of the unicameral status quo. The exchanges were quick, frank and extremely well-informed. After an hour of debate, the man in the proscenium box, disconcerted by the overwhelming applause for the man on the stage, spoke an aside: "there seemsto be," he said, "an organized claque in this auditorium".

**Raul S. Manglapus**                                           **44**

# Faith in the Filipino

The man on the stage resented the implication that the affair had been "rigged" in his favor. His eyes flashing and his nose twitching, he walked off the stage and down the aisles out of the auditorium, but not before he had shouted for all the nation to hear: "I have done more than any other President anywhere has ever done".

For he was President Manuel Quezon — and the man in the proscenium box was Juan Sumulong, the uncompromising leader of the decimated opposition.

I recall to you this great debate — however abruptly and dramatically it thus ended — because I find it doubly useful in the somewhat mixed context that events have introduced into this evening's celebration.

First it should serve to temper considerably the readiness with which some of us in this age of great debates would downgrade, by specific comparison, the maturity of our politics. Indeed, no chief of state in modern history, not, certainly, the President of the United States, has ever, while President, submitted himself to public debate with the leader of the opposition. Heads of government, prime ministers, yes, but never the head of government who is also the chief of state, and who carries in his person the very dignity of the republic. It requires extraordinary and, if you will, dramatic confidence in one's self for a President to submit himself to debate without fear of impairing the prestige of his office.

Quezon possessed that confidence. And in thus displaying it, he helped to mark our infant democracy with a very high grade of statesmanship.

But there are those who would view this picture in quite another light. Quezon, this view would say, proved that Quezon was mature but not necessarily the Filipinos. In fact, the very achievement of Quezon — his unopposed government — demonstrated the immaturity of his people.

This brings us to the second use to which we might put the story of the Quezon-Sumulong debate tonight. For it happened in the days of the Commonwealth whose twenty fifth anniversary we now celebrate. The debate and its participants provide us with a key to the character of that political experiment.

It is not uncommon even today for some Filipinos to declare themselves unenthusiastlc about the kind of preparation that we underwent in the Commonwealth. The Commonwealth, it is said, was not democratic, because Quezon was a dictator. Quezon was a dictator because he destroyed the opposition.

There is a difference, it would seem, between defeating or even decimating the opposition and destroying it by force. The Quezon-Sumulong debate demonstrated this difference. Khrushchev may exchange words with the son of Sumulong in the United Nations but I doubt whether he would exchange anything but bullets with the leader of the disloyal Soviet opposition!

But how explain Quezon's virtually unchallenged leadership? Why did opposition seem to wither and why did followers hurry to his standard at a twitch of his angry nose? Cyrano de Bergerac could not do as much, could not strike as much fear with his magnificently ugly nose — as Quezon did with his superbly handsome one.

The reason, of course, was that what the Parisians really feared was not Cyrano's long nose so much as his long sword — and what struck fear among his fellow politicians was not Quezon's bristling nose so much as his bristling mind, quick, brilliant, sharp, its parries more clever and its thrust far more deadly than that of a swordsman's point.

The opposition was not killed in the Commonwealth. It died because no one proved equal to the task of challenging Quezon's leadership. Fellow Nacionalista Osmena would have been equal but he chose to yield, not coweringly but gallantly. And even the big Democratas, Rodriguez, Recto, Perfecto chose thus to follow. Only Juan Sumulong — after Aguinaldo and Aglipay had been swept aside in 1935 — stayed on to fight for the opposition. And standing in that proscenium box at the Ateneo auditorium I saw him a lonely, but not a pitiful figure. For in his own stubborn heroic way, swamped by the applause of Quezonian admirers but not quite riddled with the bullets of a Quezonian Gestapo, he proved that the Commonwealth was indeed a genuine, albeit imperfect, democratic experience for the Filipino people.

Did Quezon's power go to his head? There is evidence that it threatened to.

But it is not for the things that almost went to his head but for those which were permanently in his heart that Quezon will be remembered. His one heartfelt passion was for the independence of his country. Today this passion has found expression in various eloquent terms in Asia and Africa. "Better starvation than slavery" said an Indian leader. "I prefer to suffer in freedom than to be comfortable in bondage" says an African chief. Patrick Henry, the American, had said it pointedly one hundred and fifty years ago "Give me Liberty or give me death".

Now Quezon was throwing it back at the Americans: "I prefer a government run like hell by Filipinos to a government run like heaven by Americans!"

"I do not mean", Quezon was quick to explain, "that a government run by Americans is always a heavenly one".

"Neither do I mean", be added, "that a Filipino government will always be run like hell."

I am certain that all red-blooded Filipinos will jump to confirm this. I am not so certain that there would be unanimity of anxiety to confirm its obverse, namely, that a government nm by Filipinos is never run like hell. Indeed it is accepted tradition for every opposition spokesman in this country to cry at the opportune moment: "Well, that is what Quezon preferred — and that is exactly what we've got! As someone put it with a tragic Shakespearian flair: "Hell may not always be with us. But in the name of heaven, must it be visited upon us with such exasperating regularity?"

My friends, so much irreverent talk can lead to gloomy conclusions, and I would warn against them. One need only look around us in Asia, and beyond Asia to the other continents of the world to see that we Filipinos possess no exclusive monopoly of the art of infernal government management On the other hand, if love of country is to be absolute and not comparative and we are not to be satisfied with sharing our misery, it is time to look for its causes and transcending partisan divisions, to attempt its elimination. There is enough to be heard and to be seen and to be verified in our society to warrant the sounding of the alarm.

By our experience with America, we were trained to believe in the separation of the executive from the legislative power. The Commonwealth Constitution enshrined this belief, establishing a Presidential instead of a Parliamentary form of national government No one who has seen parliamentary governments shake and topple all about us in Asia, in Africa and in Europe, will deny that the Presidential system, which assures us of a working executive with a fixed tenure and with direct responsibility to the people, has given us a stability which is unique and most useful. This stability has enabled us to proceed with confidence towards our chosen goals.

Indeed, it is confidence that is the mark of our constitution. But confidence — it might be asked — in whom? In all the people? In some of the people? In a select elite?

The preamble asserts that it is the Filipino people, imploring the aid of Divine Providence, that promulgate the charter. But as we read on it begins to be evident that the people figure less and less in the exercise of the power and the authority which are the main constitutional themes. The vote, to be sure, remains with the electorate, already considerably limited by voting qualifications. But there is a power gap between the bottom and the top, between the electorate and the national official. The executive and legislative officer sitting in Manila finds almost limitless power accumulated before him after every election-power to redistribute and allocate at will to the thousands of powerless communities in the archipelago.

Quezon himself was the first to recognize this. After his election as Commonwealth President, he said these words: "The Constitution of the Philippines gives tremendous powers to the President; powers that are not given by the Constitution of the United States to the President of the United States. I expect to make use of these powers, if and when it may be necessary. But I expect to use them only for the good of our people."

Herein lies the answer to the question — in whom did the confidence of the constitution-makers really repose? It reposed in the small, brilliant, corps of leaders then led by Quezon that since the end of tlie ephemeral success of the Revolution had carried on the fight for independence. It was a confidence well reposed. I think we may agree that those tremendous executive and legislative powers were in those Commonwealth days generally used as Quezon promised, "for the good of our people".

But it was a short-sighted confidence. It failed to see beyond the life spans of that corps of leaders — to prepare for the time when the demands of international conflict, of population, of new enlightenments, and new desires, would require a wider dispersal of power to permit maximum participation of the people in die political and economic development of the Republic.

It is a curious thing that dispersal of power was not really such an ugly word in recent Philippine political history. Gradano Lopez Jaena, analyzing the basic evils of colonialism, traced them to the tyranny of the few over the many, the confiscation of power from the small communities and its accumulation in the capital. The Malolos Convention yielded to his campaign and in Article 82 of the First Philippine Constitution sought, if incompletely, to erase the colonial mentality of dependence on an almighty dispositor of power by postulating the primary rights of self-government, taxation and administration in the local Corporations.

But the first Republic collapsed. Teddy Roosevelt's mischievous interim order to Dewey was, after painful soul-searching, ratified by President McKinley — and the Philippines was finally occupied by the United States. To this date, to those of us who possess the most superficial knowledge of Philippine culture and history — the figure of McKinley remains a pathetic and almost laughable one. his soldiers, after promising liberation from Spain, were reduced to "civilizing the Filipinos with a Krag" and were soon dismayed to find that this "uncivilized" nation was nation enough to produce an army that could teach both Spaniard and American a few lessons with a Mauser. And, of course; we are compelled to polite laughter at his solemn determination to Christianize a people who had been Christian for three centuries!

Is McKinley s figure really so hopeless? Perhaps not. Let us examine his actions after his melodramatic decision. Here, for instance, is something most interesting. In his instructions to the First Philippine Commission, he directs its members:

# Faith in the Filipino

"x x x to devote their attention in the first instance to the establishment of municipal governments in which the natives of the Islands, both in the cities and in the rural communities, shall be afforded the opportunities to manage their own local affairs to the fullest extent to which they are capable and xxx consistent with the maintenance of law, order and loyalty.

x x x

In the distribution of powers among the governments organized by the Commission, the presumption is always to be in favor of the small subdivision, so that xxx the Central Government shall have no direct administration except on matter of general concern".

What does all this mean? Is it possible that this "ugly American" this, if I might follow closely-contested trends, horrible, reactionary Republican, could, at the height of his imperialistic fits, display more foresight and greater confidence in the Filipino people than the Filipinos themselves thirty-five years later would dare to admit? Compare his words with these of Article VII of the Commonwealth Constitution:

"The President shall have control of all the executive departments, bureaus, or offices, exercise general supervision over all local governments as may be provided by law, and take care that the laws be faithfully executed."
(Sec. 10, par. (I).)

Consider the opinion of Constitutional experts that this provision has been so interpreted by our courts as to sanction broad executive authority over both national government departments and local governments (Fernando, Political Law, 1959, Volume II, p. 608).

Of course, this was not an original view. This was no deliberate conspiracy against the people. It had developed into a tradition since the early days of occupation when American and Filipino leaders together had produced an Administrative Code by which municipal employees and officials could be changed at the whim of provincial and national officials and by which most of the productive sources of public revenue were pre-empted by the central government so that local communities were reduced to begging for national aid.

Lopez Jaena's dream, the spirit of tlie Malolos Constitution, McKinley's injunctions — all these were rejected, and in the fever for formal independence one urgent foundation for its substantiation was forgotten — the independence of the individual Filipino, the awakening of his ancestral self-reliance.

Meanwhile, accumulation of power in the capital was breeding its natural offspring — corruption, greed, lust for more of that of which there was so much — and its spurious, more dangerous children — cynicism and despair.

Thus are the nether regions "visited upon us with such

**Raul S. Manglapus**                                    **49**

# Faith in the Filipino

exasperating regularity". Men with the highest principles and the noblest intentions succumb to the severest temptations; and we must, usually in vain, ever be searching in our leaders for heroic qualities where normal human capacities, intelligence, courage and determination should suffice. We must ever be seeking the graft-buster, the crook-chaser, the clean-up man, instead of the man with the vision, the program and the goals.

No one party, no one group of leaders can claim immunity to these temptations or perfect innocence of these sins, no one, in spite of the confidence of Quezon, the optimism of Mabini, and the faith of Rizal in the greatness and in the basic honesty of our race. For it is not that our race is so prone to dishonesty and is so incapable of quicker steps to its destiny. It is that the perils and the distractions of our chosen paths have sorely and needlessly strained its virtues and slowed down its pace.

These are some of the shackles of the past which we must shake off if we are to move more rapidly and surely into the future. It is good to know exactly what they are. It is good to know, else one begins to strike aimlessly, to dissipate his strengths. One, for instance, can go abroad and learn the useless things, the inapplicable things, waste time wishing for things that after all we may already possess.

One visits New Delhi and is there surprised that there is far less talk and evidence of corruption than in Manila — until he realizes that in that capital of a nation of four hundred million — there is far less power accumulated than that which tempts the men in the capital of this country.

One marvels at the stability that De Gaulle has given France until he realizes that what the General has really done is to separate the executive from the legislative and approximate our own constitution.

One stands in awe at German recovery and wonders why our own recovery has not been as spectacular until he realizes that what Germany has recovered from is the partial destruction of an economy that "took-off" a century before our own; until he sees that it is not so impossible for us to follow suit because German recovery has been achieved in a tradition which could now be also ours namely, free-enterprise-plus, plus imagination, plus decision, plus hard work.

I say it could be ours but it is not yet. There is yet little imagination, decision or hard work. Imagination is crazed by confusion of goals. Official decision is distracted by the temptations of office. And as for hard work we might ask the pertinent question — hard work by whom?

Government corporations are hard at work, providing jobs for political favorites, stifling private initiative, engaging in extra-curricular activities and dragging guilty and innocent alike to public ridicule.

# Faith in the Filipino

The follower-up is hard at work, amassing fortunes, seizing upon the convenient wedding of the political and economic lives of the nation, where many a progressive step forward must be accompanied with some quiet political arrangement.

Everyone is hard at work — everyone, that is, but the people.

We remember the valiant call to arms by one former President under the slogan of "Total Economic Mobilization". The call was not answered because the people had begun to look on national" economic activity as the exclusive domain of some private club — nameless but undeniable — to which they did not belong.

For even then the economic elites had begun to cluster around focal centers of political connection. And what was more fatal, the government bad not awakened to one big economic fact — that economic development, anywhere in the world, must count ultimately on the people, the people themselves to build their own roads, their own schools, to flock anxiously to instruction on the improvement of their communities, to draw forth from the soil with their own hands the wealth that God has given them. In brief, total economic mobilization needed an active and eager population, one that progress had not passed by.

One of the most impressive men that attended the conference of the Congress for Cultural Freedom in Berlin recently was a man who wishes his country to move forward by marshalling the past — the traditions, the latent initiatives that lie in the villages — and using these reconstruct Indian polity, to build a more indigenous constitutional structure that will permit all tbe people to participate in the task of national construction. His name is Jayaprakash Narayan. He went to Berlin with a knowledge of his country's past and present and thereby absorbed more intelligently the lessons to be learned for the future from the other intellectuals of the world who spoke at the conference. It is his obssession that progress in the capitals shall not pass the people by — the people in the smaller communities that make the bulk of every nation.

Is progress passing our own people by? Are we failing to harness their full potential? It took a foreign anthropologist to show me recently how this can happen. It is happening, he said, right in Manila Bay. He pointed at the fisherfolk that border the bay on the coasts of Bataan, Pampanga, Bulacan and Rizal. They have no interests in the inland; their common life is the sea. Yet they are governed locally from the inland capitals of four different provinces and by unrelated municipalities. There is no political subdivision responsive to their common interest and through which they could come alive as contributors to the national effort. In short, the life of the nation is passing them by.

The University of the Philippines Community Development

# Faith in the Filipino

Research Council has put out a report that demonstrates conclusively that the ancient self-reliance of our people is not dead. It has survived in spite of colonialism and centralism. For centuries, for instance, there has been active and uninstructed native organizational genius for the barrio fiesta. The organization is efficient, complete and effective. It has its administrative, its financial, its procurement and its operations sections. What is more important — it is native grown and is responsive to the spirit of the people.

When fiesta time comes, a citizen who has settled away from his original barrio will travel many kilometers back to participate in the preparation of its festivities. On the other hand he will have little if anything to do with the activities of his new environment. His heart is with his old community his old loyalties, and he will do anything for them.

Our municipal divisions do not exploit this spirit. Often created for political gerrymandering, imposed upon the population artificially from above, these divisions bear no relation to those natural and indigenous groupings which permit the Filipino to feel part of his community, give him that sense of belonging, and evoke his voluntary contribution to economic and political growth. There is thus a failure to harness the potential of the people.

Here, I submit, is the crucial question for our future: Will the masses of our people continue to be dead weigh which our economy must drag behind it, hopelessly retarding its pace? Or will they be a vibrant force, behind our economy, indeed, but pushing it thus forward with their own genius?

Advanced economics may afford to ignore this issue and turn their attention exclusively to more sophisticated economic theories. We may ignore it only at mortal peril to our dreams of development. Communist China has faced it, has enlisted every available muscle in her vast mainland into inhuman communes, so that her population may turn from dead weights to moving forces for her development. Surely, we can find within die spirit of our democratic society the formula that will release the forces for this transformation.

We will find that formula. We will find it if we are ready to admit mistakes, to correct imperfections, to assess our capacities, to look at the past with neither chauvinistic pride nor hasty lament but just to learn from it the lessons for the future. We will find it if we issue the call for fresh ideas conceived in freedom and examine them openly, fairly, thoroughly, ready to choose the best and carry them out, even if this means tearing down some incidental institutions which we might have mistaken for the essence of democracy.

This Commonwealth celebration should provide us with inspiration for such a search. For in 1935, the Commonwealth of the Philippines itself was a fresh and a novel idea in international affairs.

# Faith in the Filipino

The decision of a sovereign occupant to surrender a colony under pressure not of arms but of argument was even at that late period a bold and challenging concept. It pricked the conscience of other colonial powers and raised the hopes of occupied people everywhere in the world.

I have perhaps been strict in judging its accomplishments. I should therefore conclude this judgment by citing the best authority of all — the Filipino people, who rendered their judgment in blood.

There are those who would now suggest that the Filipino youth who marched to Bataan, knowing less of Rizal than of Lincoln, were moved to battle more by propaganda than by patriotism. I can think of no more vicious slur on the name of the Filipino. I think that the Filipino can feel through the fumblings, the human ambitions, the initial deceptions, the conflicts, the mistakes, draw forth the solid benefits, the promise and the substance of freedom, press these to his heart and offer to die for them.

This is what he did in 1941. And in doing so, he prescribed the posture that his country might strike for the future and before the world. It is one that is confident but not reckless, one that is aware of the limitations of size but not eager to use them to shirk responsibility for the defense of universal liberty.

We accepted this prescription — struck the posture, and not everyone has understood us for it. Let us pray that new free world leaderships, in their drive to understand neutralism, will not make it any more difficult for us to be understood; and that the avowed neutral nations may begin to recognize that it might just be our small accommodation towards the balance of power that permits them the luxury of being neutrals.

Here in this hall we might aptly re-consecrate ourselves to these responsibilities. This building was erected by Filipinos who went to America to learn, who there never forgot that they were Filipinos, and who returned to use their knowledge for the betterment of tlie Philippines. The rolls of this Association are filled with names of men who are among the most genuine nationalists of our time.

Let us thank them for this privilege of celebrating with them tonight the anniversary of the beginnings of an era of promise, of fulfillment however partial, of confidence and of faith.

-----

# IX. Desire And Choice —
# Bases For A Free Economy

**(Speech delivered before the Philippine Association of National Advertisers, Manila, January 11, 1961.)**

Since the day I was invited late last year to speak here tonight, I have taken a rather unusual step in my checkered life — I have joined an established political party.

Those of you who might be acquainted with the tortuous paths which I have followed in my rather frustrated political career will perhaps find in my joining the Liberal Party the ironic closing of a political cycle which began in 1949.

In that year, some friends of mine thought it might be a good idea to form a new party, fresh, clean, dynamic, a rebellion against the venalities of the then ruling group — the Liberals. Some of those friends you will recognize: Soc Rodrigo, Manny Manahan, Narciso Pimentel, Jose Ma. Hemandez, Jaime Ferrer, Frisco San Juan. To become our leader, a Liberal Senator bolted his party dramatically on the issue of corruption. The first president of the Citizens Party was Lorenzo M. Tanada, whom we all admire.

The Citizens Party presented local candidates for elections in 1949 and 1951. These went the way of independent candidates — i.e., they lost. In 1953 we found common cause with Ramon Magsaysay. We joined the non-partisan MPM, the Citizens Party coalesced with the Nacionalistas, Tanada was re-elected senator in the Magsaysay ticket, and we served in the Magsaysay administration. In 1957, shortly before the death of President Magsaysay the Citizens Party was split on an issue involving Senator Recto. Preferring the leadership of the President, we left the party and after Magsaysay's death and a brief service under President Garcia, we formed the Progressive Party. In 1959 we were joined by some distinguished Liberals and Nacionalistas — some of whom like Nacionalista Rodrigo and Liberal Pimentel were old Citizens Party friends — and we formed the Grand Alliance.

Today, twelve years after we issued our challenge against the Liberal Party in 1949, we ourselves have become Liberals.

There is, indeed, irony in the closing of the cycle. But, you will pardon me for adding, if there is irony there is also fulfillment.

Twelve years we spent challenging the status quo, seeking to substitute venal men with good men, corrupt government with clean government, the old with the new. But, aside from the three refreshing years of Magsaysay, it was always an elusive pursuit.

**Raul S. Manglapus**                                         **54**

# Faith in the Filipino

It occurred to us that the reason the pursuit was so elusive is that we had concentrated on substituting men instead of ideas: that we had condemned corruption in the capital and thought we had solved it by putting up an incorruptible man — until the incorruptible man died — and corruption came back. We had failed to analyze why corruption thrived in the capital and why we almost need a saint to resist it. We needed an idea on how to stop it.

For incorruptible men will die. But an idea, a good idea on how to stop corruption might just live long enough to see it stopped.

The idea that we evolved was a simple one. There is grave corruption in the capital because there is too much power in the capital. After four centuries of colonialism, we still, in our independent state, labor under a colonial system — where the concentration of power in the capital at once produces two grave tragedies: it corrupts the leadership and prevents the people from participating in the task of national development.

The dispersal of this power — a process which has produced progress and industrial power for every democratic nation that has adopted it — is the essence of the program that we thus formulated. It dawned on us that what we really had wanted to fight in 1949 was not a Liberal administration — but a system — a centralized constitutional system which robbed the people of their faith in themselves.

There was thus fulfillment in the closing of the cycle, when the Liberal Party accepted this program and paved the way for the unification of the minorities. For the Literal Party has had like the Nacionalistas, its days of temptation and of forcing the people to submit to centralized dictation. Now at last it comes to the people pledged to do away with this temptation, to restore power to the people — to revive the faith of the Filipino in the Filipino.

This will require change — not only of men but more especially of systems and attitudes. The "outs" are not trying to oust the "ins" simply to take their turn at sharing in the loot. They would like to come in and return the loot to the people.

What has all this to do with National Advertisers?

The first change that we seek is to be made in the mind of the Filipino. It is a painful change. We want to persuade him that he can improve himself, his life and his community by his own efforts. We want to change the system, so that the government, instead of restraining him, will provide him with the freedom, the incentive and the assistance to meet this challenge.

Our manifesto states:

> "The way out of stagnation and into sustained economic, social and political growth is individual hard work, sacrifice and self-discipline.
> "The new leadership does not wish to deceive our people

# Faith in the Filipino

that it can be otherwise
"On the contrary, it is its purpose by example to spur our
people to undergo those painful changes in attitudes,
values and motivations which are necessary for this growth.
"The new leadership shall by administrative action, by
legislation and constitutional amendment, by public policy,
by official and social recognition, by education and persuasion,
seek promptly to place the Filipino in a position to meet this historic
opportunity to build for himself a sturdy and vibrant society".

Gentlemen, if self-confidence is to be regained by the Filipino — if he is to shake himself and move forward — he must be unshackled by his own government, he must be encouraged, aye, tempted to improve himself by government and private incentives.

Decentralization will unshackle him, the new leadership will give him official incentives. This is not enough. In a regime of "free enterprise — plus" to which the new leadership is committed, private support is most essential.

Let me now read to you paragraphs from a speech delivered recently in London by Lord Heyworth of Unilever Limited on the subject of advertising:

> "No society can remain static; it must either progress or deteriorate. Most are striving to improve their standards of living, to reduce poverty and drudgery. How, then, does advertising help to bring about a rising standard of living? First, I suggest, by making people receptive to the idea of change, For, paradoxically, although human beings want to improve, there exists in most of us a certain inertia towards change and one of the justifications of advertising is the part which its persuasive power plays in helping to overcome that inertia and bringing people to see that the old ways are not necessarily the best ways.
>
> To take one example from our own past, one might ask what the British soap trade would be like today but for the first Lord Leverhulme's passionate belief in advertising. How much longer would it have taken to get beyond the anonymous bulk of the long unwrapped bars that were the normal form of soap until he burst upon the scene? And if the force of advertising sometimes seem to be not so much to persuade as to act as an irritant, that is not necessarily a bad thing either. Anything that attempts to change us or jerk us out of our existing habits is apt to be regarded as an irritant. Yet although a challenge to go one better than before can be an uncomfortable bed-fellow it is a prime cause of progress in every field of human life, and it is advertising that brings that challenge home to the individual."

Save for the specific reference to wrapping for bar soap, (for the original idea of which our friends from Philippine Manufacturing Company would probably like to dispute with Lord Heyworth) the

**Raul S. Manglapus**                                                           **56**

distinguished Unilever chairman sounded almost like a manifesto writer for the united opposition!

Indeed, if it is the rival claims for Lux and Camay soaps that excite the curiosity of the man in the barrio, if they spur him to test them, if they drive him to earn more, to work more, to plant more, to build that feeder road himself in order to transport those otherwise abandoned bananas to market and increase his personal income so that he may buy both bars of soap and enjoy their rival fragrances, I say let us have more of these claims, more advertising, more of these incentives for productive activity.

This, gentlemen, is economic development — basic, democratic, economic development.

There are advocates of industrialization who impugn rural development as a concurrent objective of national policy. But industry must have a market — the market is the people — and the people must have the income with which to purchase the products of industry. It is rural development that even now has pushed up the sales of basic necessities in the barrios. Wherever a feeder road is constructed and the market is made more accessible to the farmer, his income has thrice increased and the first thing that he thinks of buying more of is the very commodity that Lord Heyworth would like to sell — soap! Statistics establish that the sales of soap, of toothpaste, of soft drinks have trebled indeed in areas affected by feeder road constructions.

And what made the farmer yearn for that new soap, that novel toothpaste, that sparkling drink? Advertising.

If democratic industrialization is not possible without rural development, it is obvious that the intent of these theoretician industrialists, whose ideas sound strangely identical to those expounded by Communist Political Transmissions, is to lead this administration and our nation inevitably to socialist dictatorship, to carry out industrialization under government management by forcing the people to work for subsistence wages, to consume less than is needed for a decent existence, or, as in the extreme form of the Chinese communes, to work as slaves for nothing in anticipation of a prosperous millenium which they have no hope of enjoying.

For a socialist economy is geared to propaganda. It will produce goods for exhibition abroad — it will dump watches and bicycles at ridiculous prices to attract trade — as Red China has clone in Cambodia, in Malaya, in Vietnam — and leave the home market thirsting in vain for these same goods. In such an economy, with a propaganda market abroad and a captive market at home — there can be no place for advertising.

To quote Lord Heyworth once more "more than just business communication, advertising is essential to a free economy. A free economy presupposes freedom of choice for the consumer, just as at the other extreme a totalitarian economy restricts freedom of choice by restricting what can be chosen".

If advertising is essential to a free economy, so is a free economy essential to advertising. A controlled, licensed economy, restricting the market to licensees has less use for advertising than a truly free arrangement where the fight for the market is open and unrestrained.

It is here that our manifesto again becomes pertinent.

It says:

> "In consonance with our faith in the individual Filipino, the new leadership is pledged to an economic program that will produce prosperity for all and achieve the ultimate goal of placing control of the national economy in Filipino hands by releasing the energy of every enterprising Filipino to freely create wealth.
>
> "In place of restrictive, stultifying and self-defeating economic-controls, its pledges to provide positive guidance and incentives in the form of tariff designed to consolidate our national economic gains, credit preferences that will open up leading economic sectors to sustain economic growth; and stable economic policies."

In pursuit of this policy, we must have more than mere tokens of encouragement for advertising. For I think I do not go too far when I say that advertising is capable of proving, perhaps more than most occupations, the self-reliance of the Filipino and of restoring his faith in himself.

Oliver Cromwell once said that the public should be given "Not what they want but what is good for them". It is presumed that he intended the power to choose what is good for the people to rest in a centralized, political authority.

Advertising affirms the opposite. It assumes that the people are capable of choosing what is good for themselves. Indeed, they may, and will make, mistakes. But, if I may quote Lord Heyworth for the last time:

> "Naturally they will sometimes make mistakes, but they learn from those mistakes, and build up a resistance which one might compare to that which the human body develops from measles and other childhood ailments. As a result, they are not all that easily misled. And they are essentially human. Their lives revolve round the places where they live, their families and their homes, for providing good things for their children, dressing better, striving towards an improved standard of life. They lay great store by what they possess and what they have achieved. In these matters they have a well-developed sense of self-protection. They want to lead their own lives in their own way, and above all they want freedom of choice, including the right to make their choice, for whatever reasons seem best to them, whether they be emotional or icily rational."

# Faith in the Filipino

The more I read Lord Heyworth, the more I feel that he might have missed his calling. These words I dare say could well be the most eloquent defense of the Filipino in the barrio. They confirm his self-reliance, his capacity to choose well, to govern himself and to better his condition; qualities which have been proven by scientific researchers, such as those of the University of the Philippines Community Development Research Council; qualities which have been deniesd by some majority spokesmen, such as a Congressman who recently mocked the capacity of the Filipino and would, like Oliver Cromwell, spoon-feed the people with their every little need from an almighty depository of power.

Here, indeed, is the third freedom in a free enterprise society. If the first is the freedom for the investor to put his capital in the enterprise he deems most productive and the second, that of the entrepreneur to develop and produce the products he chooses; the third, and perhaps the most vital, is the freedom of the consumer to choose that product which suits his own needs best.

Here is the cornerstone of advertising. Here is an eminent expression of faith in the citizen.

Faith in the citizen includes, of course, faith in the advertiser himself. This means that we must trust him to keep his claims in truth and in taste. An activity so urgent to development as advertising cannot afford to be false nor to be in bad taste. Both faults do violence to national morale, to industry and to advertising itself.

Truth and taste control must be left less to law than to the advertisers themselves. In keeping with our credo, this is the manner in which all worthwhile activity must be encouraged to improve itself. Just as we believe that private education can best raise its standards by mutual, private accreditation, so do we have faith that advertisers can best do the job of self-policing and self-improvement themselves.

There is perhaps some room for action in this direction. I can see, for instance, the logic, and, if you will, the cultural consistency in a soft drink company paying for a "caratula" which reads: "Pete's Eats Drink Happy-Cola"; I am afraid I fail to see either logic or cultural consistency, however, in the sign: "Funeraria Tepok — Time For Orange Lime!'

The closest cultural justification for such a peculiar association of ideas disappeared from this country long ago with the advent of Christianity, namely, the custom of providing the dead with food and drink. And one feels that perhaps it would he more faithful and more fair to our rich cultural tradition if such extreme positions were avoided in the otherwise healthy advertising war.

The possibilities far self-discipline and cultural promotion are particularly bright in this association of the  men and women in Philippine national advertising. In your roster are names that represent

**Raul S. Manglapus**

the most educated and cultured segments of our society. The obvious and constant efforts of Philippine advertisingat improving the cul-tural content of their copy is but a reflection of the personal qualities of the members of this association.

In congratulating the officers that were inducted this evening, we might call to their attention the uniqueness and the gravity of the responsibilities that face them.

I invite them to consider that in a free society and in an industrializing economy such as ours, the word of the advertiser is becoming as important, as influential and as effective as the word of the politician in the shaping at public wants, public needs, public attitudes, public opinion, and thus in the formulation of national policy.

I invite them not to shirk the comparison but, with confidence in their capacities, to accept it and face its implications.

I invite them to be politicians, that is, to think in terms of the people and participate articulately, unequivocably in the pursuit of national objectives.

I invite them to discharge the role that the hour demands of them — to revive the faith of the Filipino in himself.

I invite them to sharpen with words of truth his desire for the good things in life.

I invite them thus to fortify the base of our industrial democracy — a people alive, desiring, working, producing wealth from their Cod-given soil, consuming the products of industry, working and producing again and again and by this unending process demonstrating the workability and superiority of a free political and economic order.

It is an invitation worth accepting, for its alternative is the death of our democracy and the triumph of slavery.

I see no choice for Filipinos whose lives are so firmly linked and whose hearts are so closely devoted to the ways of freedom.

-----

# X. Command Responsibility And Treaty-Making

**(Speech delivered before the Philippine Confederation of Professional Organizations, Manila, January 15, 1961)**

One of the first reasons why I readily accepted the kind invitation to address you this evening was my discovery that in this distinguished confederation of professionals there are no lawyers.

# Faith in the Filipino

It is not that I have no wish to mingle with lawyers. The Law, however maligned, is still a distinguished profession.

It is that being a lawyer myself, I thought it was most flattering that an organization of professionals from which lawyers have been excluded should think of inviting me into their midst. I felt I should take advantage of the opportunity of mixing with the members of this justifiably exclusive aggrupation of citizens.

For lawyers are not always to be found in the most exclusive circles. One recalls the occasion when St. Peter and Satan were having a heated dispute over the boundary of Heaven and Hell. It seems that Satan, true to his wily ways, had succeeded in furtively pushing his border fencing forward inch by inch until, when St. Peter discovered it, he was already squatting on quite a bit of heavenly territory.

St. Peter was, of course, incensed with holy anger and demanded that Satan move his boiling cauldrons back to within properly infernal bounds. Satan, however, would not budge. And since St. Peter was committed to non-violent methods, he finally threatened Satan with the following words:

"If thou dost not retreat to thine own territory, I shall sue thee in court!"

Whereupon, drawing himself up to his full triumphant height, and crossing his arms in the most devilishly confident air, Satan replied:

"Go ahead and sue. Where art thou going to get a lawyer?"

It would seem, my friends, that there are at least two exclusive circles where lawyers are not admitted. While I naturally hope to break the tradition and eventually get admitted into the one, you will understand why I am quite excited about being admitted now into the other — the Philippine Confederation of Professional Organizations.

Of course, I suppose we lawyers could break down the barriers of the organization by sheer force of numbers, there are so many of us. Yet, unlike other professionals were not even good for export. One young Filipino entrepreneur who does business with Vietnam said to me recently: "We're recruiting doctors, engineers, nurses and other technical professionals but we have no use for lawyers."

Indeed, there is increasing interest among professionals in the search for employment abroad. There seems also to be some concern about the entry here of foreign professionals. In fact when I was approached by your President about this evening's speech, he transmitted to me the request of your membership that I deal with the coming and going of professionals, with particular reference to the Treaty of Amity, Commerce and Navigation which has just been concluded between Japan and the Philippines.

Seeking to comply with your request, I attempted to obtain the official text of the treaty, which is the only sound basis for any discussion of its provisions.

The official text is not available. It is classified information. The government has said that it would like public discussion of it but continues to withhold the subject for discussion.

Failing to obtain the official text I thought that then I might get the official interpretative comment. There is none. There is no official comment because there is no official stand.

Speaker Laurel last Thursday delivered what I am told was an able defense of the treaty before Manila Rotary. But his, apparently, is to be taken as only one administration view.

There seem to be quite a few of these administration views. Malacanang has almost sotto voce declared the treaty to be "satisfactory".

The Foreign Office which was quite obviously bypassed in the negotiations is silent and we must presume that it is adopting the graceful posture which it has struck on most major issues of foreign policy and foreign service lately namely: "watchful waiting." (It is said that if the American State Department under the late Mr. Dulles is to be credited with the original policy of "brinkmanship" for pushing the U.S. to the brink of war, our Foreign Office today must be credited with the original policy of "watchmanship" for pushing the nation to the brink of a nervous breakdown with so much "watchful waiting"!)

The Secretary of Commerce is reported to be against the treaty, while his Undersecretary is very much in favor.

The Chairman of the Senate Committee of Foreign Relations has urged caution and is not ready to submit the treaty for ratification.

Never has there been so much confusion over such a vital document as a treaty. One looks in vain for responsible leadership, for some traces of responsibility in command to guide the people in the consideration of its merits.

The administration would like to know where the people stand on the treaty. I think the people are first entitled to know where the administration stands. Does it really want to push the treaty? Or was it merely pushed into negotiating it by political expediency?

Friends, it is here that there is pertinence to the issue of command responsibility. I think that I might be forgiven if I read to you what "Faith in the Filipino", the manifesto of the united opposition, has to say on the subject:

The new leadership will assume full responsibility for the condition of the state and the conduct of government.
"It will not seek to evade responsibility for the malfeasance of one

official by attempting to dissociate itself from the perpetrator.

"Neither will it cover up by pointing to another official who may appear to be performing his duties.

"Our Constitution provides that tile President, and no one else, is the Executive. All other officials of the Executive department exercises delegated authority and arc mere extensions of the President's personality.

"Therefore, while he may not Ire held criminally or legally responsible for the misdeeds of his appointed assistants, he is not exempt from moral and political responsibility.

"Therefore, the President may not retain a tax-evading cabinet member nor refuse to prosecute him for his evasion on the ground that it is not the President's own act and thus not his concern. Worse, he may not justify this evasion by pointing to the activities of another cabinet member who appears to be discharging his normal functions of seeking out tax evaders but whose eyes are strangely blind to the evasion of his fellow officials.

"This is the principle of COMMAND RESPONSIBILITY.

"It applies to the President for the conduct of national affairs, to the Secretary for his department, the director for his bureau, the Chief for his division, the Governor for his province, the Mayor for his city, the Municipal and Barrio officials for their local administration.'*

It applies, I will add, to every important activity of administration — most particularly to a treaty into which we have entered as a sovereign nation.

We are left with little guidance, and must shift for ourselves. There are unofficial texts available, the provisions of which might conceivably be contradicted in an official text. But let us take that chance and see for ourselves what these texts have to say on the matter which most concerns this organization — the entry and local practice by foreign professionals.

The two pertinent paragraphs are the following:

"1. Nationals and companies of cither Party, within the territories of the other Party, shall be accorded treatment no less favorable than that accorded to nationals and companies of any third country with respect to all matters pertaining to the levying of taxes, access to the courts of justice and to administrative agencies, the making and performance of contracts, rights to property participation in juridical entities, and generally the conduct of all kinds of business and professional activities." (Article II, par. I, Treaty of Amity, Commerce and Navigation between the Philippines and Japan)

"4. With reference to the provision of Article II, paragraph I, relative to the grant of treatment no less favorable than that accorded to any third country, cither Party may require that such treatment shall be dependent on reciprocity with respect to the enjoyment of rights on immovable property and of the right to practice the professions." (Paragraph 4 of the Protocol)

# Faith in the Filipino

It seems to me that in assessing the merits of these provisions, we must not lose sight of two valuable yardsticks: the first is the interest of our national economy in general; and the second, the interest of the Filipino professionals.

Our country holds the distinction of having more degree holders per capita than any other country in the world except the United States. We have the largest entrepreneurial and technological base in Southeast Asia. For our industrializing economy, all that is lacking is for some of this base to be refined through training arrangements with the United Nations, the United States, the Colombo Plan and friendly industrialized European nations.

Specific industries, however, will require a substantial volume of skilled labor who are below the professional level and who obviously can not be trained in general training programs. For this is sometimes becomes necessary to permit the entry of skilled technicians from abroad to train local labor. This is already being done today on a contract basis and at the instance of established business and industrial institutions.

Unless the professionals of this country see any great possibilities in general practice in Japan, I would suggest, *mutatis mutandis,* and assuming all the other provisions of the treaty to be acceptable, that implementing legislation be passed taking advantage of the reciprocity clause in paragraph 4 of the Protocol, to limit the entry of Japanese professionals to those under contract for specific periods for the instruction of skilled complements in local industry.

I frankly see no prospect of exportation on any appreciable scale of our surplus of doctors, engineers, nurses and other technical professionals to Japan. Japan herself is not lacking in these categories. And the language barrier will be quite insurmountable.

No particular service would therefore seem to be rendered to Filipino professionals by these treaty provisions. But the Most Favored Nation Clause could reassure the Japanese about the treatment of their technicians who come into this country for the instructional purposes which we have described. Whether such a reassurance is necessary is difficult to say. Even without a treaty, there have been a substantial number of such entries upon application of private firms. I must admit, however, that during my tenure at the Department of Foreign Affairs there was always some fuss about admission or extension of stay of some Japanese technicians. Perhaps legislation in implementation of this treaty would serve to regularize the process.

Is such a benefit of sufficient magnitude to justify the whole treaty?

To answer that question we must examine every provision and that is not our objective this evening. But that and other questions, indeed, remain to be answered.

**Raul S. Manglapus**                                                    **64**

# Faith in the Filipino

For instance, it is alleged in defense of the treaty that it is the best obtainable now. Not enough has been said. it seems to me, to show that such a treaty was needed at all now. The Japaneae panel in the Reparations negotiations wanted the Philippines to commit itself to begin negotiations on a trade treaty within a month after the signing of the Reparations Agreement. The Philippine panel did not accept this suggestion and the agreement carries only a commitment to negotiate the second treaty in the future without any commitment as to the time of negotiation.

In the light of this, it seems that the burden is on the administration to demonstrate not only that this was the best obtainable treaty, but that this was the most propitous time to negotiate such a treaty.

Until this and other difficulties are answered — and I am for giving the administration the opportunity to get itself organized at last and provide the people with authoritative answer on them — I see no hurry for blanket condemnation of the treaty.

But if the public is to be informed and to form its opinion for legislative guidance these things must first be done:

1. The official text must be declassified and released to the public.

2. The Secretary of Foreign Affairs, as the official government spokesman on foreign policy, must take a well-defined and unequivocal public stand. "Watchful waiting" might possibly be justified as an attitude towards developments abroad — but it becomes ridiculous when taken towards a treaty that one's own government has negotiated.

3. The Chairman of the Committee on Foreign Relations of the Senate must after, and not before, officially endorsing the treaty for ratification, call for public hearings.

This is the proper and only manner in which a responsible administration should deal with a treaty by which it seeks to commit the entire nation on a permanent basis. It seems to me that only Speaker Laurel has the courage to defend his own treaty. The others are indulging in the good old convenient operation — passing the buck.

Ladies and Gentlemen, treaty-making is a serious affair. But if careful study precedes negotiation, I see no reason why boldness and imagination should not characterize official attitudes in specific instances.

I am, for example, rather excited by the idea of regional arrangements to promote economic development. There have been a few proposals by private businessmen in this direction, notably by my friend, Hilarion Henares, Jr.

The basic idea would be, as in the Henares proposal, to begin with a group of nations possessing certain cultural and facial bonds, geographically proximate and with similar but not entirely identical economic complexes. The Philippines, Malaya and Indonesia seem to fit such requirements.

There would then be formed a Pan Malayan Common Market similar to the two European groups now existent, and propelled by the same economic imperatives such as broadening of the domestic market which operated to seal the final union of the original thirteen American colonies.

It is not my part to improve on Mr. Henares' own excellent public exposition of this idea. I would like to stress the special significance which such a move might bear for Filipino professionals.

Any device that would stimulate national economic growth would, of course, ultimately benefit professionals in this country (even, I must admit, lawyers) in the form of expanded opportunities for private practice.

But there are even more immediate benefits possible in this instance. In all of Asia, there is a lack of degree-holding professionals. The obvious prospects of such a situation for a country with a surplus, like the Philippines, is being demonstrated in Vietnam.

Filipino doctors, engineers, architects, veterinarians, nurses, surveyors, dentists, technologists, beneficiaries of universal education and victims of national economic imbalance could almost immediately find practice opportunities in other Asian countries, whether Malay such as Indonesia and Malaya, or non-Malay, such as Burma, Cambodia, Thailand, India, Ceylon and Pakistan.

Treaties may not even be necessary, when the receiving country is ready to accept Filipinos without reciprocal arrangements, such as Vietnam.

A condition for such a program more fundamental than written treaties is that the Filipino be understood and appreciated in Asia. No amount of formal documentation will bring this about. Before the Filipino is completely accepted as a helper of others he must be known as a helper of himself.

This means that the Filipino must first demonstrate his ability to keep his own house in order. Cultural understanding is essential and cultural exchange must be undertaken. I have personally been privileged to be participant in organizations that have assisted in this direction. But this will take time.

It will take time before our fellow Asians fully understand why we dance to semi-Spanish folk music, why we follow Christ instead of Allah. But something else can more quickly seize the imagination of these young, struggling nations — the success of another Asian nation in establishing for itself a stable, democratic political economic and social order.

In the whole of Asia — and many Asian intellectuals have

begun to accept this — the Philippines is gifted with the most promising basic materials to ensure this success — a political stability, a forward cultural outlook, a substantial and vibrant middle class, and limitless natural resources.

Asia is waiting to see what we do with these materials.

If we are content with our gains, if we close our eyes to the grave defects of our political system, if we are happy with an unsolved problem of recurring corruption at the capital and a mentality of dependence among the millions in the rural areas — that Philippine status quo of which Asians are growingly aware — we will have failed ourselves and our hopeful, waiting neighbors.

If we seek to move forward, if we open our eyes to ideas not only for a change of leaders but also for a change of system—changes that will redistribute power, reduce temptation at the capital and restore the faith of the Filipino in himself, if we can thus mobilize our human and material resources in order to outpace the increasing demands of population and ideological conflict, if we can prove that an Asian country can remain free and still achieve economic sufficiency — then no Asian will think of refusing our friendship, our cooperation and our commerce. For no one will refuse another whom he admires.

There is, if I might be colloquial, something in this for professionals.

There are incalculable benefits, immediate and long range.

But there is also work — hard work by the professional as citizens — full, alert participation both in the dialogue and in the mechanics of building a strong, democratic society.

The Filipino professionals are second in number in the world. I am confident that they will be second to none in their response to this universal challenge.

-----

# XI. Industry, Culture And Policy

**(Speech delivered (in Tagalog) at the Awards Presentation, Filipino Academy of Movie Arts and Sciences, Manila Hotel, March 3, 1961)**

When I was in Berlin last June to attend a conference I received a telephone call from Mr. Ingles, our Ambassador in Bonn. He was most upset because Manny de Leon who was supposed to head the Philippine delegation to the Berlin Film Festival had cabled in the eleventh hour that lie could not come.

Could I please stay over in Berlin after my conference and substitute for Manny?

# Faith in the Filipino

I explained that the German government had already arranged an official tour of Germany for me and I could not possibly postpone it.

"But", Mr. Ingles pleaded, "it would be a service to the country."

I replied that they also serve who travel and learn, especially at the expense of another government.

The argument went on for sometime until the good Ambassador, feeling perhaps that the long distance call was beginning to assume costly proportions, decided to use one final desperate, but telling, argument.

"But, Mr. Manglapus", he said with a most appropriate tone of voice, "think of all the international movie beauties that you could meet!"

The record shows that I did not stay in Berlin and that I resisted this final appeal to my aesthetic emotions. And my appearance here this evening demonstrates that while I might resist meeting international movie beauties, I cannot, I will not give up the opportunity of being with lovely actresses of our own Philippine screen.

To me they are so much more attractive than their international counterparts. They are so much more unspoiled, so much more natural, so much more approachable, so reflective of the happy, harmonious, at once quiet and dazzling blend of cultures that is ours.

Furthermore, they are possessed of one distinctive quality of which foreign beauties are not and which at the moment I find completely irresistible — they can vote in Philippine elections!

Ladies and gentlemen, I have tried to follow tradition this evening. I have begun my speech with an attempt to make you laugh. I have done this against the advice of a friend. He felt that since I would speak on Filipino movies, I should instead begin by making you cry. Thus, he said, I would immediately get into the spirit of the occasion, because that is all a Filipino movie is good for — to make you cry.

There are only two kinds of Filipino movies, my friend said, and they both make you cry — one kind because they are so sad — and the other because they are so bad.

Being a good friend I tried to give his advice a receptive ear — until I asked him when the last time was that he had seen a Filipino film and he answered; "Not so long ago — 1929!"

It is evident how much Filipino movies have improved since then. They have ceased just to make you cry. They make you laugh, they strike fear, they keep you in suspense, they arouse all the other noble emotions of which the human soul is capable. In brief, they are mature. They are products of the genius, the hard work, the desire for perfection of those who act, direct, produce and participate in the many important activities that contribute to the creation of moving pictures.

This maturity has reaped honors in regional festivals, it has yielded distinguished by-products such as the formation of the Filipino

# Faith in the Filipino

Academy of Movie Arts and Sciences. It has given us the glitter, the dignity, and the fulfillment of this night.

Indeed, the time for crying is past. Yet, there seems still to be room for some sorrow.

I say there is room for sorrow because while motion picture production has become a first class Filipino industry, it occupies a definitely second class position in the hierarchy of Philippine values.

I do not refer to the fact that Filipino pictures are not shown in first class theaters. There is already a Manila ordinance which would require first class exhibitors to show local films at least once a month. I am told that no Philippine producer has ever taken advantage of it because a local picture in a first class theater would not last more than one day due to a "minimum daily receipts" rule.

I refer first of all to the attitude of the government itself.

The government seems intent to make motion picture production as difficult as possible. It has singled out the industry for a unique "gross tax", which levies on the producers' gross receipts whether or not the picture makes any profits later. And any net profits are of course subject to the usual taxes.

This gross profits tax is a tax on capital. Because of it the producer is beaten before lie starts. It lessens his capacity to invest more in better scenery, better salaries, better quality for his picture. The producer, in the eyes of the law, and standing beside his fellow Filipinos who are engaged in other industries, is thus reduced to a second class citizen.

But in other countries, he would not be thus reduced. In Indonesia, in Turkey, in Sweden, in Switzerland, in Japan, in Belgium, in England, in Denmark, in France, in Spain, in West Germany he would he a most privileged citizen, favored by governments that appreciate the special role of the motion picture producer in the economic and cultural development of the nation. There he would enjoy either government subsidies or tax reimbursements or foreign exchange preference or reciprocal arrangements which would enable him to compete on fair footing.

But here, in the land of "Filipino First" he is the Last Filipino. For instance, a government that has sworn not to recognize or trade with Communist countries has permitted Communist pictures to come in and offer him competition. No Communist books for our young, no Communist guns for our soldiers, no Communist shirts for our workers, no Communist propaganda for our people! Ah, but Communist movies! That is different. Let's bring them in just to make life little harder for the big, bad Filipino producer, and for his evil co-workers — the Filipino actor, director, cameraman, script writer, et al.

Tagalog? Let's spread it! It is our strongest hope for national unification. Let every man, woman and child speak it at home, in the market, in the office, in the street. Teaching it in schools is not enough to achieve this. The Filipino must learn to hear it, enjoy it, speak it outside the classroom. Tagalog movies! That will do it! Let us make it easy for the producer to turn out more Tagalog pictures. So let us tax his raw film, let us tax his processing, let us tax him on footage, let us tax his gross, let us tax his net — let's really help him. It's a good cause!

Foreign exchange? We need all we can get. Our films are actual dollar earners and potentially could earn much more. They are in demand in Asia and even now are being contracted for in art houses in the United States. So let us make it cheap and easy for our local producer to film and export and compete abroad. Let us fix it so that while the Japanese can export a color print to Indonesia for only $1,000.00, our producer must, because of taxes spend P5,000.00 just to make one, and spend some more to get it to Indonesia. That's the way to help him — squeeze the blood out of him and then make him fight!

Ladies and gentlemen, it is no wonderthat  our motion picture industry, receiving such a second class treatment, finds it difficult to maintain its first class spirit and attain its first class objectives. It is caught in the maze of contradictions that is the character of government policy today.

Policy must be reoriented so that vague slogans give way to concrete steps towards the strengthening of the faith of the Filipino in himself. And it is not just the faith, the self-reliance of the man in the barrio that must be revived. It is also the faith and the self-reliance of the Filipino middleclass, of the entrepreneur, of the industrialist whose desire to plan, to work and to produce finds little encouragement in an atmosphere where pull, not planning, influence, not work, are the recognized prerequisites for productive enterprise.

I suspect that this is exactly the way the Filipino film producer is feeling today. He is of the pioneering class, who dared to enter the field of production at a time in our history when the foreigner was presumed the only one capable of managing the production not only of films but of any other product for manufacture in this country. When he started, there was little official interest to encourage him. He worked hard and he looked forward to the clay when an independent government might, with deeds and not with words, support him in his struggle to prove the ability of the Filipino in this important field of production.

And this is what his waiting has yielded — a government of catchy slogans but stifling laws, of many flags waving, but of so little done to fire the honest, the hard-working, the intelligent entrepreneur to produce his best for the national economy.

Evidently, the victim must soon break free of these shackling deterrents to his productivity. He will know how to do it when the hour comes.

But the final victory for the Philippine movie industry will not come simply with a change of government attitude. Final victory will come only with some basic alterations in the thinking of our people.

A moving picture is an animated reflection of life. It is thus the most detailed reproduction that is possible of a culture, a civilization, a way of living.

Many Filipino films are even now per se first class. But the Filipino film industry will never truly attain first class status until our people begin unanimously to think of our own culture as first class.

The battle for this prized attitude must be fought on the intellectual plane. There the enemy is not the government, not the competitor, but the Filipino who would like his fellow Filipinos to think that we have no worthwhile culture at all, that we have emerged from our colonial experience with a culture impoverished rather than enriched by the influences that have touched our islands. Such a man would have us cast away whatever was not "originally" grown on our soil and by this process arrive at the "true" culture of our people.

His most interested and active ally is the Communist organizer who would be most happy to see created in this country a sort of a cultural vacuum so that he might fill it with a new substance carved in the Marxist-Leninist fashion.

Ours is a culture of many layers. Our shores have been overwhelmed by the tides of invasion of many forms and intensities.

The original Malays that bred our basic race came to these island by sea some centuries before Christ. This was thousands of years after the first men had come on foot or on the backs of their work animals over the land bridge that once connected us with the Asian mainland.

Once the Malay had settled, his native customs, his traditions, his beliefs, his language began to develop and to grow with accretions from many sources: the Chinese, who came mainly to trade; the Hindu, whose impact was mainly cultural, the Muslims, whose influence was borne to us from Java and Sumatra on the arms of the Madjapahit and Shri-Visaya empires; the Spaniards who came to conquer and convert; the American who sought to redeem his earlier confusion with a benevolent regime.

I have just been to one of the great sources of our cultural enrichment — India, that limitless subcontinent of four hundred million people, at once victim and absorbent of many military and cultural invasions.

There I was put in personal touch with customs that might provide the explanation for some of our own — family cohesiveness, spirituality, hospitality. As I dined on hot curry food with Indian friends, I was reminded that our "achara" is their "achar", that our "mukha" is also their "mukha" — and what is even more significant — our imparter of knowledge, our "guro" is also their "guru". We were amused by the fact that our fruit "atis" is inverted in Hindu into "sita" — which led us not without laughter to conclude that the Indian is nothing hut a Filipino upside down, or vice-versa!

There are limits, of course, to our similarities in cultural development. India's geographical position is in the middle of the Asian mainland, herself radiating mysticism and in turn being swept by the mystic winds of other Asian lands. We face both Asia to the West and the Pacific to the East, and the cultural winds that have swept our land after the Indian influences of earlier centuries have been somewhat different — Latin Christianity from Spain, a forward, private enterprise democracy from America.

The distinctness of this culture can no longer be denied. The world has accepted it in applauding our artists, our dancers, our lecturers and our writers abroad.

The potentialities of this culture lie in its very hybrid nature. It is the hybrid cultures of the world that have achieved real greatness. Such, for instance, is the culture of England.

Why do I stress all this today? I stress it not only to persuade our people of the richness of our culture and thus to elevate in their estimation the mission of the Filipino moving picture as the mirror of that culture. I stress it also to persuade the moving picture producer himself that therein may lie the key to building up a truly great movie industry.

How often have we heard it said with a sigh that all the Filipino film industry needs to achieve a permanent place in the international market is one, just one truly great picture, one picture to win world awards and universal acclaim.

I know that this picture will be made — but when? Not, I humbly submit, when we shall have collated enough capital and equipment to rival the colossal productions of Hollywood. Not when we shall have succeeded in aping the stark-realism of the post-war Italian film, the open suggestiveness of the French, the cleverness of the British, the technique of the Japanese, the unique mystic quality of the Indian.

That one great picture will be produced, and here, if I may dare to suggest, are the steps to its final production.

First, we must be convinced of the greatness of our culture.

Second, we must be convinced of the industry's mission as the reflection of that culture.

Third, we must strive to make the industry a faithful reflector.

Fourth, we must study our cultural past, our present position, our distinct historical role in Asia and in the world.

Fifth, we must choose from this context a theme of

contemporary value albeit of centuries-old vintage. Such were the qualities of "Rashomon" and "Pather Panchali."

For instance, in a world taken up with the problems between East and West, where is the Filipino film that has depicted the conflicts and compromise between East and West not only 011 Philippine soil, but more important, in the Filipino soul?

In a world concerned with revolutions for national freedom and with the rise of new nations, where is the Filipino film that will, with humility but with sincere pride, remind the world that the first successful national revolution outside Europe and America, was the Philippine revolution of 1896 and that the first republic in Asia was the Philippine republic of 1898?

We will produce that one great picture — if we are faithful to our heritage and proclaim our pride in it. We need have no fear that we will not be believed. To reassure us, let me reiterate what I said upon my return from Europe last year:

"In one of the great European capitals I was taken to see a hall of fame. 'There', my distinguished guide pointed out, is a poet, here a linguist, this one a novelist, that a physician, he a sculptor, this a dramatist, now a historian, this a man who inspired our revolution, and that a man who died for his country.'

"'We have no wonderful halls of fame such as this', I regretfully admitted to my host. 'But then', I said "it is perhaps because with one statue we could have all that we find here. There was one Filipino who was all this — poet, novelist, sculptor, biologist, physician, dramatist, linguist, historian — who inspired our revolution and who died for his country. His name was Jose Rizal'.

"'Yours must be a great race', said my host, There is no equal figure in the history of Europe.' "

My friends, an Indian diplomat who has stayed in the Philippines and who was impressed with our cultural optimism, put it to me this way in New Delhi last month: "You Filipinos are the coming race."

This, I submit, is enough material to make one great motion picture. It is also enough material to build one great nation.

The men and women of your industry in making the one, will be building the other. That is how important your role is in the great drama of our history.

-----

# XII. Private Initiative And National Health

**(Speech delivered at the National Convention, Philippine Medical Association, University of the Philippines, Quezon City. April 28. 1961)**

Ever since I accepted the kind invitation to address you this morning I have had the strangest feeling that I have allowed you to make a most unhappy choice of speaker.

You have asked me to give you a layman's view-point on a medical question. The difficulty is that I am not an ordinary layman. I am a lawyer — and a lawyer cast in a hall full of distinguished doctors of medicine must by definition be overcome with a strong inferiority complex.

Furthermore, I am not exactly the kind of average layman that makes the ideal subject for statistical polls, particularly on an issue between government and private initiative. I am a layman obsessed, you might say driven with an overpowering sort of faith — faith in the Filipino.

Recently, I had occasion to collaborate in writing this faith down as a political manifesto. Permit me to quote a pertinent portion:

"Next to faith in God and in our nationhood the most fundamental belief required for democratic national development  is the faith of the individual citizen in his capacity to contribute to that development.

"The beginning of nationalism is faith in one's self, in one's ability to work with his fellow citizen in the building of the nation.

"The new leadership proposes to revive this faith. It proposes to do this by proclaiming and implementing its own faith in the Filipino, in every Filipino worthy of the name, no matter how humble his social class or economic resources.

It believes in a nationalism that is truly national, a Filipinism that embraces all Filipinos."

When one believes in such a faith, it is obvious that he must resist every government attempt to do for the citizen that which the citizen can do for himself. It is obvious that one would then stand squarely against government action which would stifle ready, eager and capable private initiative.

One would then do battle with paternalism, that evil which is one step from socialism, which in industry makes management treat laborers like children and which in government makes it seek, like the mother hen, to cover every citizen with its protective wings — for so long and so thoroughly that the citizen is finally smothered to death.

# Faith in the Filipino

This is not to advocate the return of "laissez faire , that extreme "hands off" position, which can result in economic confusion and disorder. This is to ask the government to abandon its mother hen posture and be more like the realistic father who lends his son capital, gives him encouragement and incentives and lets him out on his own.

There are those who supporting private or voluntary health insurance today would seek to soothe the feelings of the supporters of government action by adopting this compromise attitude: no socialized insurance today — maybe later when we have national discipline.

I cannot go along even with such a compromise attitude for several reasons.

First, it assumes that the Filipino people are incapable of national discipline today. It is at least debatable, it seems to me, whether or not we Filipinos are not already possessed of the degree of discipline necessary for our present needs. I do not think we suffer too much in this respect in comparison with some Asian, Latin American and even European countries that I have seen.

Second, it assumes that socialized medicine is the ideal thing in admittedly disciplined countries. I have been to England, and I did not feel that unanimous enthusiasm for the system which its advocates seem to assume prevails in that country; and of course the other supposedly top — disciplined country, the United States, is very far from even adopting the system.

Third, it suggests the most dangerous corollary attitude that national discipline of the highest degree is a consummation devoutly and relentlessly to be pursued at all cost. Such an attitude would render our people perilously amenable to the short-cut, the quick, regimenting action from above, like the national-socialism of Hitler and like some of the excuses for parliamentary democracy which are being foisted on some Asian peoples around us today — the short-cut at the expense of human dignity.

High national discipline that is in keeping with human dignity is a good thing. But it cannot be imposed from above. It cannot be reached simply by preaching it. It must come from the people themselves. In this country it must begin with the citizen shaking himself from his lethargy, with the citizen getting into action, ambitioning, working, building. National discipline is impossible in a passive people. Only the awakened and the self-reliant are capable of self discipline. A passive people can be aroused momentarily to violent revolution. Soon after they will slip back to their passivity. Only an active people can go on to build a free and strong republic.

In countries where people remain passive, there is continuing lamentation over colonialism, whose centralized tyranny choked the initiative of the people. It seems to me that there is not enough lamentation there and in this country over the continuation of this tyranny of centralism in our own independent constitutional government.

The heavy hand of over-centralized government continues to strangle the self-confidence of the people in the smaller communities, continues to compete with private initiative, discourage the professional, harass the businessman and confuse the educator.

And while this destructive process is going on, a parallel play is put into operation. The monstrous government enterprises, spoiled children of centralized power, are manipulated to squeeze from the citizen every possible drop of blood for the blood-bank of the political campaign. I am not indicting any particular party or any particular official. I am indicting a system which has lent itself to these grotesque and inhuman practices by the tempting proportions in which it permits the accumulation of power.

Mr. Chairman, I am told that the general proposition of this morning's session could be broken down into specific issues, such as, should the GSIS build and operate its own hospitals. I suggest that there are issues before us that are deeper than that. I suggest that it is most pertinent that we consider not only whether government institutions, like the GSIS, should expand their operations but whether they should continue to exist in their present form at all.

And, if we are to assume that we are a democratic republic and that therefore the government exists for the people and not the people for the government, then I suggest that the burden rests on the government to justify the continued existence of these massive institutions.

It is not enough that they establish that they are not losing money. Proof that they are making money is merely evidence that there is good business to be had --- it is not evidence that the government should indulge in it and that private enterprise is not ready to undertake it.

No less than the distinguished secretary of this association has told me that in spite of GSIS health insurance, public school teachers, for instance, take out voluntary health policies because of their more attractive terms. I am assured by private insurers that their aggregate force could undertake the insurance functions of the GSIS today. In the face of this situation, the GSIS must show why it should continue to deprive companies of legitimate business and the government employees of the obviously better service that private insurance companies can offer.

Before discussing whether the GSIS should build its own hospitals, I submit that there could first be fruitful discussion on why the GSIS does not think of using the same amount of money to give out loans to private hospitals to permit the expansion of their facilities for the care of government insurance holders.

# Faith in the Filipino

I am not an anarchist, my friends. I believe in government. I am proud, and I have proclaimed this pride abroad, of the stability of our presidential system. But I am ashamed of our over-centralized, all-powerful national government and I am suspicious of every attempt to extend its tentacles into more and more sectors of human activity. I believe in the capacity of our people in our communities to solve, given authority and support, their own problems.

I believe in every Filipino. I have respect for the Filipino medical practitioner. I believe in his ability, in his patriotism, in his willingness to cooperate with his colleagues in the extension of medical care to as great number as possible of our people, if only the government would support and not stifle his initiative.

I believe in his ability to organize efficient hospitals. Given government capital support, he can set up new ones or widen the activities of the present ones to supply the services that the government now insists in giving directly.

There is great noise over Filipino First. The greatest competitor of the Filipino is his own government. Filipino bankers, for instance, are ready to dominate local banking operations. But the Philippine National Bank, its pioneering days long over, continues to control more than half of the business, to the disgust of private bankers but to the joy and profit, particularly at election time, of the party in power.

And now comes this — not just an over-extension of a defunct pioneering function — but a new incursion into fields where private competence has been brilliantly demonstrated: medical practice, hospital management and health insurance.

Where the need is to unshackle the citizen from the chains of a colonial mentality of dependence, there is here a move to forge the chains even more securely. Where the need is for freedom, there is here the promise of bondage.

Let me conclude by clearing up a misconception of the role of socialized action in England. England is consistently referred to as the model of a democratic socialism. England, my friends, has progressed, as the ex-Socialist Max Eastman has said, in spite of, not because of socialism. It was her tragic flirtation with socialism after the war that caused a victorious England, in spite of her industrial potential, to be overtaken by a prostrate Germany which recovered at phenomenal pace by staying on the speedier steed of free and private enterprise. England now proceeds more speedily with the non-socialist pattern of the ruling Conservative Party.

I pray that this docs not happen here, that our efforts to take those giant strides towards economic stability are not smothered prematurely under the solicitous wings of an officious government.

My friends, ours is a rich culture, a wealthy land and a forward-looking race. Let us give these assets a real opportunity together to

**Raul S. Manglapus**                                                    **77**

fashion a great nation by releasing the spirit of the Filipino into the stimulating air of competition, work, incentive and faith.

Faith in the Filipino — this is the key to our nation's future.

-----

# XIII. Spanish—Language of Oppression?

**(Speech delivered (in Spanish) at the Cursillo of the Division of Spanish, Phil. Normal College, Manila, May 11, 1961)**

While eating some hot curry food with an Indian friend in New Delhi recently, we talked of the cultural and linguistic links between India and the Philippines. We discovered that our "achara" is their "achar" our "mukha" is also their "mukha" and what is even more significant — our word and theirs that denote the imparter of knowledge — the teacher — are one and the same "guro".

As we had dessert, we recalled that our fruit "atis" is in Sanskrit inverted into "sita" which led us laughingly to conclude that a Filipino was nothing but an upside down Indian and vice versa.

But when the conversation turned to the deeper aspects of our cultural outlook some hard conclusions had to be made. Although both Asians, although both sharing in many ways the ancient Hindu culture, although both touched, if differently, by the Anglo-Saxon, one by the reserved Englishman, the other by the eager American, there was no denying that we looked at many things in entirely separate ways.

We both agreed that the answer was not to be found in this country — that the differences in cultural outlook between the Indian, the Indonesian, the Burmese, the Malayan, the Vietnamese on the one hand and the Filipino on the other was to be found in earlier times, in the basic difference between the colonial policies of England, Holland and France on the one hand and Spain and Portugal on the other.

The British and the Dutch came to Asia to trade. Being anxious to trade, they did not bother with attempts to transform the culture of the colonial population. Thus the noted British historian Christopher Dawson writes:

> "Western colonialism and Christian missionary action are two distinct forces, even though they are interrelated, and the former achieved its greatest success only when it had disassociated itself completely from the latter, as the Dutch and the English East India companies both did in their palmy days. It is well-known that the Dutch retained their trade with Japan only by disassociating themselves entirely from Christianity, hut it is

even more significant that in Ceylon they took deliberate measures for the restoration of Buddhist monasteries by importing reformers from Arakan in 1684 in order to weaken the existing native Catholicism.

"In the same way, in India, the East India Company, far from acting as an agent of Christian propaganda, originally prohibited any missionary from entering the country and contributed to the maintenance of Hindu temples and the celebration of religious festivals like the great Jaganath pilgrimage of Puri".

France undertook a measure of the missionary effort. But Spain and Portugal, particularly Spain, inflamed with the missionary spirit and at that time knowing only one way to Christianize, namely, by first Hispanicizing indigenous cultures, transformed the cultural content of their colonies. That is why we find pagodas in Burma, mosques in Indonesia and baroque churches in the Philippines

By royal decree not only were our first names Christianicized but our surnames were sought to he Hispanicizcd, a process which, due to several circumstances, was not fully accomplished.

This, of course, made it a most natural thing that the indigenous mind should begin to think in Castilian terms.

The process of Hispanization was carried out most effectively by the system of education. In the sixteenth century, the first universities of their kind outside of Europe were already functioning in Manila, promising to build a new Spain in Asia.

But the new Spain was not built in Asia. It was built in the vastness of South America.

The Castilian language in the Philippines was the language of the ilustrados, of the educated middle class, of the centers of concentrated Spanish influence, such as Manila, Cavite and Zamboanga. But as the erudite Encarnacion Alzona admits in her "El Legado de Espana a Filipinas": "Es bien sabido que la hermosa lengua de Cervantes no llego a ser idioma comun en estas islas."

If the transformation of Philippine culture is a phenomenon in Asian colonial annals, the strangest aspect of that phenomenon must be that the transformation was achieved without the acceptance of Spanish as the national language. Three and a half centuries of colonization did not achieve the thorough Hispanization of the Filipino tongue. The indigenous languages flourished in the rural communities even as Spanish was taken into the hearts of the city folk, the professional and the aristocrat. The epics of Balagtas were not written in the pre-Spanish era. They flowed from his pen when the Spaniards had been governing his people for almost 300 years.

I mention this in order to challenge those who accuse the Spaniards of deliberately limiting the knowledge of Spanish to a few select Filipinos, so that, as the charge goes, the majority might be prevented from reading liberal literature from abroad.

What is truly indigenous can never be uprooted. In Latin America, where because of massive immigration from Europe, Spanish finally became the national language in every country except in the former Portuguese colonies, the native languages of the ancient kingdoms are not dead. Only a few miles away from Mexico City there is a community that speaks nothing but its ancient Aztec tongue. This is true in many places in Peru, in Bolivia, in Paraguay, in Brazil, in Guatemala. Spanish reigns in the nation. But in the small community, there still reigns the ancestral tongue.

But, of course, this is true in Spain itself. It was a surprise for me last year to hear not Castilian but Valenciano spoken by my friend, Don Tomas Morato, to his neighbors in Javea, to enter a book store in Barcelona and hear not Castilian but Catalan over the counter. This is true in other countries of Europe. I heard a sermon in Patois, a curious combination of French, Latin and Italian in the south of France. In Britain, English will never supplant Welsh in the Welsh miner's home.

But there must be a national language. And as in Latin America, even without the massive immigration, it might have been Spanish in this country. Certainly the spirit, if not the letter, of the Spanish tongue was already in the national soul. Perhaps, if its progress had not been interrupted at a time when modern universal educational methods were being born, we would today have no more debates on the national language.

Even from the viewpoint of physical adaptability, Spanish is a better medium for our people than English. Like Tagalog, Spanish is read and pronounced as it is written. Our oral muscles lend themselves much more readily to its pronunciation; a distinguished former American rector of the Ateneo recently admitted to me that it was a mistake for the American administration at the turn of the century to change the medium of instruction from Spanish to English. Aside from the reasons above stated which he also cited, he felt that continuity was broken and it led to the language confusion that we suffer today.

But, of course, that was perhaps too much to expect of an ebullient, victorious Uncle Sam! Furthermore, the insistence on English was not without its reward. We are now in close touch with the accepted new lingua franca of international relations.

That is where Spanish went. Now, where does it go from here?

A placard carried by a demonstrating student at the Congress recently denounced Spanish as follows: "Spanish is the Language of Oppression."

No doubt, my friends, you who love Spanish, who know better what Spanish meant and what it did not mean to the Filipino people and to Filipino culture, were justifiably incensed by such an irresponsible and inflammatory charge. No doubt you would like to get hold of that student, comer him in a room, and remind him that if the revolutionary spirit was against the colonial policy of Spain, it was not against her culture and her language; that the literature of the revolution, the propaganda of del Pilar and Lopez Jaena, the manifestos of Mabini, the novels of Rizal, the decrees of Aguinaldo, the Malolos Constitution, were all written in Spanish. In this same literature, in this same tongue, the leadership of the revolution gave vent to two violently opposing emotions: hatred for Spain's colonial policy and love for her culture and her language.

If Spanish was the language of oppression, if its spread in this country meant the suppression of our indigenous culture, how did Balagtas write Florante at Laura, not in the original script of the ancient Tagalog, but in the Roman letters and with the Roman flair which his genius of a mind had acquired from his Spanish teachers at San Juan de Letran?

If Spanish was the language of oppression, why, after Spain had gone, would Palma, Apostol, Guerrero, Recto continue to express in it their yearnings for a great nation in this land?

In recent history, there have been two kinds of men who have subscribed to this charge. First, there was the over-zealous, excited American administrator who inspired, not without reason, by his own sense of mission — and in many ways as misinformed as his President who thought of Christianizing a nation more Christian than his own — saw nothing in the Spanish era but darkness and oppression. And today, there is the leftist organizer, who by perpetuating the canard that our culture was totally destroyed, not just transformed, by Spain, seeks to create a sense of vacuum in our culture so that we may begin to judge our history and our behavior in Marxist-Leninist terms.

Yet, one cannot entirely blame that placard-bearing student for allowing himself to be thus misled. He is a young man almost completely cut off from the Spanish traditions in our culture and sees in the learning of Spanish nothing hut an added burden in a curriculum already crowded with many government requirements.

In helping him solve his problem, I do not propose to go into such details as how many hours of Spanish studies he should undergo. I propose, instead, that we reexamine our whole attitude towards the teaching of Spanish today.

What are our objectives? In the light of the fact that Spanish was the language of leadership but was not the national language, are we adjusting our sights so as not to overshoot our target? Are we planning Spanish studies in such a manner that we resist the temptation of putting it in a place in our culture in which it never was?

We are today carrying out an educational program which

interprets the original American idea of universal education in massive terms. Ours is no longer an exclusive school system. Many of our students in Manila and most certainly in the provinces come from families whose historical contact with Spanish has not been on the elevating cultural level that was to be found in the universities, in society and in commerce, but on the harsh, sometimes degrading level of social relations with the Spanish encomendero, who often might have exemplified in his behavior the less desirable aspects of Spanish colonial policy.

You love Spanish. It has been to you a source of spiritual elevation. How much of this love can we expect for the language from those who may view it from a radically different point and who may associate it with far less elevating memories?

Here in Manila, there is an Alliance Francaise and a Goethe House which foster the French and German languages. In this country, these tongues, unlike Spanish, are not handicapped by confused past-colonial sentiments. Yet, in introducing each language, care is taken so that first there is developed in the student an affection for French or German culture.

Are we not taking things for granted with regard to Spanish? Arc we rushing to compulsion, provoking a misunderstanding of motives without first considering whether there might be need to foster affection for a culture and a language which has meant so much to the enrichment of our own culture, our own tongues and our own lives?

I speak perhaps in paradoxes. Why indeed, must a people have to learn to begin to love a language that has meant so much to them? But the truth must be accepted. The millions of our people — and this is the admitted target of your present Spanish educational program — are no longer in contact with the strains of Spanish tradition in our cultural pattern. They must be reminded that to know the real Rizal one must read him in the original. And to read him in the original one must read Spanish. They must be reminded that our forward attitude today, so different and so much more optimistic than those of peoples around us, is due in great measure to that invigorating cultural potion which we unbilled in the cup of the language of Cervantes. They must be reminded not to throw away this boon, this precious link with almost a third of the people in the United Nations — all former colonies of old Spain.

Of these and many other things about Spanish our people, our students could first be reminded as a reintroduction to the language. I am not asking that the Spanish educational program be scrapped. I do ask that it be reviewed, that the motive of affection be fostered and be permitted to supplant the coercive requirement for passing a school year.

In brief, I am asking that in pursuing this educational program, we create lovers, not haters of Spanish.

This perhaps could he achieved by exploiting the voluntary good will of the present lovers of Spanish. Beneficial legislation could bb passed to encourage the formation by private groups of a national institute which could be in contact with and receive support and encouragement from their counterparts in Spain and Latin American countries. This institute could establish centers all over our country, fostering affection for the language, while the schools keep up with their teaching of it in keeping with the increase of this affection. The private aspect must be emphasized. The elements of free voluntary action must be stressed to overcome the necessary coercion of a curricular program.

My friends, there are three realities in our language picture today.

Tagalog is tlie basis of our national language and it is here to stay. Just as Castilian is the national language in Spain, Hindu in India, English in Britain, although regional tongues in these countries arc fostered, so will Tagalog be the expression of our national soul, even as we encourage Ilocano, Pampango, Visayan and other regional dialects.

English will stay as our second language. We will do well to keep it so, unless we arc ready to throw away this advantage that we possess in our contacts with the outside world which today also provides us with a provisional lingua franca within our borders.

Spanish is deeply rooted in our culture. But even as it is so rooted, the leaves and the brandies are today paradoxically not aware of it.

It is your mission to awakenthis awareness, to set the record straight, to clear the air of historical error, to do battle with the extremist and prepare the way for the restoration of affection for the language.

Many are the judgements that have been passed on the record of Spain in the Philippines. What better judges are there than our revolutionary leaders themselves who rendered judgement by fighting for liberty while swearing their love for the culture of Spain? And what better immortalizer of such judgement than the artist who lived with those leaders and was in the vanguard of the revolution himself — Juan Luna y Novicio?

In his painting "Espana guiando a Filipinas en el Sendo del Progreso" which Alzona reproduces in her "El Legado", Luna pictures a far different Spain than that which today's extremists would paint for us today. There she is a gentle matron, embracing Filipinas and walking with her on the road to progress.

The perfectionist would perhaps not accept the maternalistic accent of this picture today. He would perhaps rather have Spain and the Philippines walking hand in hand and helping each other as partners to progress in this atomic world. Today's Spain herself might perhaps profit from an exchange of views with the Philippines on such questions as the problem of civil liberties.

But the judgement is there — the judgement of a contemporary — and I suggest that it be accepted.

You who love Spanish must rebroadcast this judgement. It is the only way by which your love, so justly nurtured, can begin to be shared by our people. I congratulate you that you should be faced with so noble a task.

-----

# XIV. A Selection of Short Talks, Statements and Other Papers

## *1. Heroic Leadership — Its Temptations, Its Checks*

### STATEMENT ON
### "DEMOCRACY AND HEROIC LEADERSHIP
### IN THE 20TH CENTURY"
### A PAPER DEFENDED BY ARTHUR SCHLESINGER JR. OF
### HARVARD UNIVERSITY CONCRESS FOR CULTURAL FREEDOM
### BERLIN, JUNE 17, 1960

I should like to add a few thoughts to those brilliantly exposed in your paper on the reconciliation of heroic leadership and democracy.

I note that you include in your enumeration of the heroic leaders of the 20th century the late President of my country, Ramon Magsaysay. I am wondering whether we might draw from the Philippine experience under Magsaysay some partial answers to the questions which you have posed.

You have said, sir, that heroic leadership can lead toward democracy or away from it — depending on what the leader does with his power, and what his people permit or encourage him to do. This, perhaps, is the key statement in this important portion of your paper.

Ramon Magsaysay became a leader of heroic proportions after successfully defeating a Communist rebellion as Minister of Defense. He became a hero both because he crushed the rebellion and because of the means which he used in crushing it. In the process of crushing it, he made the people, both the overwhelming majority loyal to the democratic cause and the discontented minority who rebelled, feel important. He resettled the captured rebels in their own independent farms on public land. And he reminded the nation that political power lay not only in the city intelligentsia and middle class but also in the people in the barrios or Philippine villages. On this platform he was elected President.

By turning the eyes of the people away from the promises of the Communist leadership in the hills of Luzon back to the leadership at the Presidential palace, Magsaysay might be said to have been playing a dangerous game of substituting the promise of centralized authority with an actual one. Indeed, for a while everything seemed to be concentrated on his personality. But he resisted the temptations that you mentioned as attendant in such cases. He did not extend the crisis artificially. On the contrary he certified to Congress measures of legislation which would grant greater autonomy to the barrio governments and bring to the surface the latent initiative and self-reliance of the smaller communities which had been left out of the stream of government activity since colonialism introduced a highly centralized system in the sixteenth century. After his tragic death in 1957, these measures finally became law.

This answers the question, "What did the leader do with his power?" But the other one which you ask remains. If Magsaysay had chosen to do otherwise would his people have permitted or encouraged him to do so? The answer to this was given by our people way back in 1934 when they passed a constitution which makes it most difficult for any leader, however laden with charismatic qualities, to perpetuate himself in power or to transform the character of the republic. We had, from the time the American occupation began at the turn of this century to the time of our independence, a 76-year experience in the separation of powers, which in independence takes the form of the Presidential system. No one may dissolve the Congress and the President's power are independent of those of Congress. The people elect the President directly for a definite term. The President can only push constitutional amendments by three fourths majority in Congress or by Constitutional conventions and by majority ratification by all the people.

Finally, there is suggested in this example, an answer to the perennial question about heroic leaders: "After him, who?" or worse, "After him, what?" Magsaysay died in a tragic plane crash in March, 1957. Vice President Garcia immediately was sworn in as President in accordance with the constitution. There was much lamentation but no one challenged the new President's right. It was all in the system, and two Presidents had died before.

I do not aim to oversimplify nor do I suggest that this example could be of universal application. I do agree with Maritain that crises will demand heroic leadership and we might successfully minimize the attendant temptations to such leadership by a proper choice of system.

## 2. Can Democracy Work In Asia?

### PUBLIC SYMPOSIUM SPONSORED BY
### THE INDIAN GOVERNMENT,
### NEW DELHI, FEBRUARY 7, 1961

Intellectuals today are sorely tempted to conclude that democracy is not working and cannot work in Asia. Western-style democratic institutions implanted in that vast continent are finding in the problems posed by underdevelopment a challenge of a magnitude which they never faced in the countries in Europe and American where they were originally evolved. For the moment the record, viewed from the average, is not impressive. In some instances, the situation may be called critical. And it is from these critical examples that one is tempted to conclude that democracy is failing.

This alleged failure of democracy is explained by some as the result of the imposition of alien Western-grown institutions on Asian societies. There is fallacy and oversimplification in this explanation. Democratic institutions, wherever grown, are freely evolved human institutions. There are directions in the evolution of every civilized political organization which are necessarily similar because of certain universal qualities of human society. Before Spanish colonization in the sixteenth century, the communities dotting the Philippine archipelago enjoyed local governments in which the executive, legislative and judicial functions were clearly marked even though they might have been discharged by overlapping bodies. The national legislature, the chief executive, the Supreme Court cannot be called alien to any human organization. The smallest corporate structure, whether political or commercial, will contain these functions and officers in some form and name.

The introduction of the so-called "Western" institutions should, therefore, not necessarily do violence to Asian politics. On the contrary, where properly introduced in transitional periods, the result can be political stability. This, I think, we can claim for our own country, where after over forty years of constitutional experience, we now enjoy as an independent nation a stability known in very few other places in Asia.

But it is a fact that these traditional constitutional weapons, whether in the Presidential or Parliamentary form, cannot by themselves suffice to fight the grassroots problems of underdeveloped and thickly populated nations. To solve these problems, these forms must now be given massive indigenous substance.

This substantiation can be achieved by the revival of the self-reliant spirit of the native village. This spirit has been doused by

**Raul S. Manglapus**                                              **86**

centuries of the centralism introduced by colonialism and perpetuated in many independent constitutions. This is no mere rhetorical eulogy of the barrio, the panchayat, the village. In the Philippines, scientific researchers have rediscovered for cynical politicians to see the reservoir of initiative and vitality that lie latent in our barrio people.

The secret of permanent and rapid political and economic development does not lie in the destruction of democratic institutions, whether "borrowed" or native. On the contrary, it lies in the preservation of these and in their strengthening by the stimulation of active, mass popular participation in their functions. Military interregnums and "enlightened" dictatorships may see unstable nations briefly through specific political or economic crises. But the long term answer to the challenge of new freedom is the maximum voluntary participation of the people in government. Asian democracy must be guided in this direction. If it follows this road, it will succeed in Asia and Africa as it has succeeded in the West. The alternative is forcible participation and the destruction of liberty.

## 3. No Taxation Without Participation!

### MANILA
### AUGUST 5, 1961

No taxation without participation!

This is the cry I have taken up in behalf of the people in the barrios and municipalities of the Philippines.

I invite you to join me in this cry.

When you buy a bottle of beer you pay 15 centavos in tax, when you buy a pack of cigarettes you pay 24 centavos tax, when you buy a can of kerosene you pay ten centavos tax and when you buy a bar of soap you pay three centavos tax.

For every item we buy for our daily needs such as sardines, clothing, soft drinks and other things we pay taxes almost all of which arc sent to the national government in Manila and placed at the disposal of Congress and Malacanang.

A single barrio of poor people pays thousands of pesos a year in taxes this way. When you want some of this money back to pay for improvements in your community you must go to Malacanang and beg for that which comes, after all, from your own pocket.

Even if the law provides for some allocations for local governments from national funds, Malacanang can withhold and delay their release. You have to bargain away things, including perhaps your votes, in order to get what is rightfully yours.

Furthermore, huge banking and financing institutions are under the control of the President — the Social Security System, the Government Service Insurance System, the Development Bank of the Philippines, and the Philippine National Bank. These institutions command millions and millions of pesos of public funds.

The President also, personally or through his secretaries, has power to appoint many local officials, chiefs of police in cities, municipal treasurers, all public school teachers, health officers, etc.

The sum total of all this is the most extensive power placed in the hands of any chief of state or national legislature. In 1905 President Quezon said: "Theconstitution of the Philippines gives the President of the Philippines more power than that which is given by the American constitution to tire President of the United States."

The immediate effect of this tremendous concentration of power and money is temptation — almost irresistible temptation. The next step is graft. The next is bribery. The reason why there is so much stealing in the national government is because there is so much to steal.

If you need a loan from the government — you will get it if you are ready to pay pabagsak or bribe money.

If you need money for your feeder road — you will get it if you are ready to go to Malacanang and kneel down and exchange your political support in return for money that comes from you.

Since almost all power is in the hands of Malacanang and Congress the people are at their mercy. The people lose their interest in government. The people lose their faith in themselves. And national progress is very slow.

We Filipinos have reason to be proud of our country. God has given us abundant wealth in our lands and waters. We have a rich culture. We have had a glorious history of struggle for freedom and peace. And we have had great heroes to lead us in these struggles.

This heritage should inspire us to build for our Republic a future where all Filipinos shall enjoy material contentment.

But first there must be change — change in leadership, in governmental system and in the attitude of our people.

The nations that have succeeded in progressing rapidly are those that enjoy three advantages, namely:

First, their leaders inspire the people to help themselves. They do not use their power in order to make the people entirely dependent on them as they sit in the capital city.

Second, their system of government is decentralized. The smaller communities have the power to govern themselves. They use their own tax money for their own economic and social development. They do not have to beg from the national government to return some of their own money so that they have new feeder roads, schoolhouses, health centers and public buildings. The national government comes to their support in the bigger things that are required for their development, the highways, the hydroelectric projects, the big flood control and irrigation dams.

Third, the people are consequently self-reliant. They have faith in themselves. They develop the courage to go into their own ventures in order to extract from the soil the wealth that God has given them and process it for the enjoyment of every citizen.

I have been to the United States, to England, to Australia, to Germany, to India, as guest of their governments. These countries are great democracies. In these countries the people participate directly in the benefits from their taxes. The tax money that they need remains in their own communities.

This is the reason why their small communities are alive, dynamic, progressive. Each man and woman eagerly contributes in work and money to the building of the nation.

The first result, of course, is — less corruption because of less power and less temptation for national officials.

The second result is the self-reliance of the people.

The end result is progress — progress and wealth not just for a few, but for all.

This is why America is great — why Canada, Australia, and India are becoming great — why England and Germany continue to be great.

This is what we intend to bring to this country — a program of decentralization of government powers.

We will be a great country. Our lend is rich, our culture is brilliant, our women are beautiful and our men are strong.

We will be great — if we make the changes so that we can — all of us — work for that greatness.

The Barrio Charter is a step in the right direction. But we must do much more.

We must fight for greater participation in national funds.

We must fight for automatic release of allocation of national funds to local governments.

We must fight for the transfer of the power of appointment of local officials to local governments.

We must fight to restore the Faith of the Filipino in himself.

No taxation without participation!

I am running for the Senate under the United Opposition to achieve this end.

In supporting my program, my party and my candidacy, you will be supporting yourself, your barrio and your people.

# 4. Seconding The Nomination of The Vice-President

CONVENTION HALL
STA. ANA, MAKATI
JANUARY 21, 1961

I am just a new Liberal, Mr. Chairman, and it would perhaps be far more prudent for a new soldier like me to stay quiet in the ranks, to listen and to learn.

I feel, however, that I might be forgiven for presuming to speak a few words in support of the nomination of Mr. Macapagal.

Mr. Chairman, the air this morning is heavy with the spirit of victory. It is undeniable in our faces, in our words and in our hearts.

But there is another spirit which now stalks this convention hall which I hope in our enthusiasm we will not ignore. It is this spirit which consolidated our will to win.

I refer, Mr. Chairman, to the spirit of sacrifice.

We have seen this spirit materialize this morning in many golden forms.

We have just heard a brilliant young politician propose for nomination to the Presidency the very man whose ascendant leadership has stood in the way of his own legitimate ambition for that exalted office.

We have just heard, keynoting in challenging terms the theme of this convention, another young leader whose qualities hundreds of thousands of our countrymen only recently considered worthy of that same office and who has given up the leadership of his party, however modest in dimension, to become a simple follower in this one.

These, Mr. Chairman, have been difficult sacrifices to make. But they have been made in the name of unity. The people have asked for a united opposition. We have given them one — and they have applauded.

I am certain that in this convention hall there are hundreds of other sacrifices in many varied forms that are even now being undergone, sacrifices which we may never hear manifested as eloquently, but which in bitterness will equal those that have been made on this platform. Indeed, even outside of this convention hall, there are those who are making sacrifices for unity in their own way, whose sincerity and self-denial time will recognize.

One might ask at this point — where is the sacrifice by Mr. Macapagal himself?

Mr. Chairman, the hour has demanded a leader and it has produced one. The leader must lead, must symbolize the new-found union in his person. He cannot be sacrificed.

# Faith in the Filipino

But Mr. Chairman, Mr. Macapagal will not be without his sacrifice. Before unity was scaled, he accepted a proposal for a new and drastic approach to the problem of clean government and rapid national development. He agreed to reduce the powers of the President and redistribute them to the people through their local governments, thus minimizing temptation at the capital and reviving the Faith of the Filipino in himself.

Mr. Chairman, Mr. Macapagal is the first candidate for President in our history that goes before the people committed to reduce his power for the sake of the people. It was not difficult for us, convinced as we are of its validity, to make the proposal. It was not easy for him who should be soon enjoying the heady wine of accumulated power, to accept it.

This, Mr. Chairman, I submit is self-abnegation of the highest possible order in the framework of our democratic society: to seek power for service; to seek power only to restore it to its rightful owner — the sovereign people.

Finally, Mr. Chairman, I am attracted by one more quality in Mr. Macapagal. One may twist his words and succeed in making him look a poor framer of foreign policy pronouncements. One may send vilifiers on his tail, put words in his mouth, distort his pledges for responsibility in government command and succeed temporarily in ridiculing him before the people. But someone has yet to disfigure truth, falsify the record, and make of him a dishonest man.

For it cannot be done. Mr. Macapagal has had his days of power as an elected official in the years of Liberal predominance. He could have taken advantage of the conveniences of power — the controls, the influences, the patronage. He could have enriched himself. But he did not. Mr. Macapagal is an honest man.

Honesty and self-sacrifice. Are these not, Mr. Chairman, the marks demanded of the new leadership by the excesses of the times?

Honesty for that quick relief, and self-sacrifice for that permanent solution to the tiresome and demoralizing barefacedness of thieving officials and to the apathy and despair of our people?

Indeed they are, Mr. Chairman. And it is for this reason that I am proud, in the name of the men and women who have found new direction to their desire for service under the aegis of the Liberal Party, to second the nomination for the Presidency of our Republic, of the Honorable Diosdado Macapagal.

# 5. Nationalism and Hypocrisy

### MANILA
### SEPTEMBER 4, 1959

The Nacionalistas of today insist that nationalism is the issue these coming elections. All right, let it be the issue. Let the people decide who are the true nationalists who express their love for country in deeds, and who are the hypocritical nationalists who express themselves in loud slogans that are implemented in reverse. The Nacionalistas of today shout "Filipino First," but by their immoral example, by bribery and by influence peddling, they are placing the aliens more firmly in control of our economy than ever before.

The control of alien middlemen of the buying and selling of our farmers' produce could be finally destroyed by the cooperative and credit operations of the ACCFA. The ACCFA was a creature of the Magsaysay administration. The ACCFA Law was written by a member of the Grand Alliance, Vicente Araneta, and originally implemented efficiently and effectively by one of the candidates of the Grand Alliance, Osmundo Mondonedo. It was well on the way to putting control of the tobacco, palay and corn trading in the hands of Filipinos. But again, the immoral example at the top has permeated to the bottom and the ACCFA irregularities are now resulting in restoring the aliens to their former position of strength in this important sector of our economy.

The Nacionalistas shout "Filipino First," hoping thereby to hide their anti-nationalistic operations. By this, they pretend to be encouraging the strengthening of Filipino businessmen. I will not answer this ridiculous assertion in my own words; I will let the Filipino businessmen themselves, who are supposed to be the beneficiaries of this hypocritical policy, answer it in their own words.

The official voice of Philippine business is the Chamber of Commerce of the Philippines, which is headed by Marcelo Balatbat as its President, Ramon V. del Rosario as its Vice-President, and among whose directors are Jose Y. Orosa. Gaudencio Antonino and Manuel Lim. Here is what "Commerce, the Voice of Philippine Business." the official publication of the Chamber of Commerce of the Philippines, has to say in its editorial of May, 1959:

"What exasperates businessmen these days is the fact that white most of them are honest and are disposed to conduct their business above board, red tape and the intervention of crooked officials have made it almost impossible for them to do business in the manner they are used to before controls.

"In many instances several palms have to be greased before

papers could be processed and given due course.

"Taxes, fees and charges have become the subject of shady negotiations between payers and officials in the revenue-producing offices with a great deal of money going into the pockets of unscrupulous officials, and not to the government. Transactions that should not be countenanced are given official blessings for a fat fee. Transactions that are on the up and up do not go through unless bribes reach the proper parties. Almost anywhere one turns today he has to grapple with the ubiquitous influence peddler and crooked and unashamed officials.

"It is under these circumstances that all sorts of fixers thrive. And one of the bitterest indictments against the administration is that it is lending itself to the perpetuation of venalities which enrich government officials and private citizens close to the administration. In an atmosphere such as now prevails, it is the business community that bears the heaviest burden. That is why, much against the will of honest businessmen, some have been compelled to pay the services of influence peddler who abound under the present dispensation. It is most regrettable that the moral decadence is depriving the business community of proper incentives that are so necessary for the development of competent and honest business executives. For the truth is that the deplorable conditions require a minimum of competence and a maximum of shady dealings. These practices must BE stopped at all cost in order to arrest the alarming rise of immorality in and outside the government."

The Nacionalistas are the worst anti-nationalists of our day because they are destroying the initiative of Filipino businessmen. They are putting honest Filipinos out of business and forcing established Filipino firms to violate their own conscience in order to survive.

Our people largely continue to live with the same mentality of dependence under which their forefathers lived in colonial days. Many of them are unwilling to help themselves. Their self-reliance has gone, not because they are lazy, but because of the colonial type of government under which we continue to live even if we are independent.

The men responsible for this colonial mentality of our people are in the Nacionalista Party, or allied with the Nacionalista Party. We had a splendid opportunity upon the enactment of our Constitution to change this mentality into one of self-reliance and self-dependence. But the very men who want to be called the "nationalists" of today are responsible for enacting a constitution designed to keep the people under complete subjugation of political machines in an over-centralized government. By this measure these so-called "nationalists" are the most destructive anti-nationalists of our time.

The Magsaysay administration was well on the way to breaking this colonial mentality by such movements as the PACD, which restores the self-reliance of our barrio people. Today, the PACD is emasculated by lack of administration interest and understanding. Last year, the Philippines failed to live up to its full commitment for community development. The result is two-thirds of our community development program was paid for with foreign aid.

Nationalism is in deeds, not in words. The present administration cannot carry out the nationalism of deeds of the Magsaysay administration because by its immeasurable corruption it has wrecked the machinery of nationalism begun by Magsaysay. It is time for us to rise against the anti-nationalists and bring down this most anti-Filipino administration of all time.

## 6. The Mindanao Develojnnent Authority

### ATENEO DE DAVAO, DAVAO CITY
### MARCH 19, 1961

It is time to impress upon these and the rest of our country's youth, that they are heirs of an attitude that is today the mark of our race. Arnold Toynbee, the noted British historian, sets us apart from the rest of Asians because of this attitude — the outlook, he says, which is the fruit of the blend of many things — the genius of the Malay, Catholicism and our constitutional experience with America. He readily identifies this attitude — it is optimism.

It is with this optimism — and not with the despair preached by some of our own fellow countrymen, especially the Communists and their party-lining friends, that we should face every problem of our nationhood.

It is with optimism, not despair, with love, not hate, with the ambition to build and not to destroy, that you must, for instance, approach the gravest problem of our time — the economic development of our country.

The narrow, primitive view that economic development is the exclusive concern of the economist, the business administrator, and the industrialist and that, consequently, commencement exhortations to this field of activity should be limited to graduates of business, commerce and economics, is of course, no longer to be accepted. The nature of development and, indeed, its urgency in Asia now demand the energies of every citizen. Each one of you here tonight, graduates, parents and friends — whether you are or will be a lawyer advising and creating business corporations, an industrialist conceiving, financing and organizing plans for the extraction and processing of the wealth of our resources, an engineer implementing these plans, a doctor keeping men and women fit for work, a farmer providing industry with raw materials, a scientist discovering new industrial methods and new products, a businessman stimulating the marketing of these products, an office worker keeping commerce in motion, a politician stimulating industry with prudent leadership and wise legislation, or a priest educating all these and radiating to our people that self-discipline indispensable to progress — all of you have an eminent role in this development.

And it is here in Davao, here in rich, beautiful, virgin Mindanao where this development promises such dramatic strides. But too long has the bureaucracy and the leadership of an over-centralized government prevented you here from taking these strides. Too long have politicians who know little of your problems, who love and understand Mindanao much less than you — too long have these men sitting in Manila, some of whom perhaps have never been in Mindanao — too long has our system allowed them to make decisions for every step that must here be made.

A national government which truly seeks rapid development in this area should think in these terms: the key to development is the participation of the people. How much are the people here allowed to use their own development?

To put your development in your hands and thus speed up the process that will enable the millions of our impatient people to receive their share of the benefits of an expanded economy, I propose the establishment of a Mindanao Development Authority.

This Authority would be financed by an appropriation from that portion of certain Internal Revenue taxes paid by individuals and corporations doing business in Mindanao, supplemented by local taxes the power to levy which could be given by law to provinces, municipalities and barrios of Mindanao.The Authority would be governed by a Board, not appointed from Manila but nominated by Mindanao citizens' organizations and chosen by an assembly of local officials of Mindanao. The Authority would have ample license to survey the potentialities of this great island, to select which agricultural, mineral, industrial and power projects to undertake always with the view of providing the power, the incentive and the assistance to privately capitalized industry. It would have in its program the attraction of capital from elsewhere in the Philippines and if this is not sufficient from outside the Philippines for investment in Mindanao.

This is the rapid, the intelligent, the efficient, the democractic way in which regions of such progressive countries as the United States and Australia have been and are being developed. I stress that it is democratic because the key to its success is local initiative, the interest, the thinking and the labor of the people themselves.

There is need to stress this, there is urgency to this distinction, because we are offered elsewhere another method by which to employ this key to our survival  this total participation of the people. Elsewhere, as in the China of the Reds, the people indeed participate, in mass agricultural and industrial projects, not by their initiative but by the force of Communist arms, husband tom from wife, parents from children, in order with their bare hands to enable their country to take those giant "leaps forward toward the Marxist millenium.

It is within our power, within the genius of our people, within the ken of our outlook of optimism, to take these leaps forward without giving up our liberty and our God.

These young ladies and gentlemen of the Ateneo de Davao today stand ready, educated, primed and, I am sure eager for this initiative. If their initiative, if your will 'here and not those of a few almighty men in the national government is allowed to prevail — we shall soon see Mindanao developed as she should be, rapidly, intelligently and without sacrifice of democracy — providing our Republic with that substance of freedom which so many still miss so sorely in their daily lives.

This, if I might suggest it, is your mission, my young friends. May our leaders permit you to carry it out. And may God give you courage in its discharge for the sake of freedom and happiness in our time.

## 7. *Work A Year With The People*

**TESTIMONIAL DINNER**
**YOUTH VOLUNTEERS FOR MANGLAPUS**
**COLUMBIAN CLUB, MANILA**
**MAY 27, 1961**

Three hundred foreign young men are giving up the comforts of their home to live and work with our people. I wonder how many of our own youth are willing to do the same for our own people.

Will the Filipino youth permit a foreign peace corps to answer the challenge of Rizal ahead of them?

Malitbog, Bukidnon, a remote municipality is without the services of a doctor. The abandoned population is ready to pay for the living expenses and modest salary of any young graduate doctor even an intern, who may wish to stay with them at least a year.

Inquiries were made with one of our medical schools. The. reply was that no one would be interested because all the graduates were planning to work in the United States.

I am not against our professionals seeking specialization abroad. What I am against is the ambition to make a living abroad when there is work to be had here, the drive to minister to other people's needs while those of our own go unattended.

The only nations that are great are those which helped themselves. It is tragic that while American youth are giving up their comforts to work with our people, our youth are thinking of leaving our people to seek the comforts of America.

I therefore propose the organization of "Work A Year With the People" where our young doctors, nurses and other professionals will be encouraged to work for a period of one year in remote areas where their services arc needed. Each worker will be substituted by another after one year.

May I also take this opportunity to explain the Liberal program of decentralization and "free enterprise — plus". In every country there should be a party of tradition and conservatism and another party of change. The Nacionalista Party, being the older party, heavily laden with tradition, is discharging in this country the functions of the former. The Liberal Party, younger and less traditional, represents the party of change.

Sometimes a people may wish to return to conservatism after change. We can cite the instances when the Republicans have been in power in the United States and the Conservatives in England.

But at other times the people and the country's welfare may require that the party of change be given power. It is the situation in the Philippines today.

# 8. Decentralization and Command Responsibility

### KNIGHTS OF COLUMBUS COMMUNION-BREAKFAST, BAGUIO CJTY
### MAY 7, 1961

President Kennedy's assumption of personal responsibility for the Cuban fiasco is a shining example of command responsibility.

When some people wanted to shift the blame to his subordinates and even to his predecessor. President Eisenhower, Mr. Kennedy refused to blame anyone but himself. This is a lesson in democratic leadership that deserves the attention of the administration in this country today.

What is happening in the Philippines is the opposite and that what we are witnessing here is passing-the-buck, command irresponsibility and command indecision.

The party in power answer charges of corruption by trying to resuscitate similar charges against the old Liberal Administration but it shows neither the ability nor the desire to admit responsibility and correct its own faults and crimes.

Mr. Kennedy's example also refuted eloquently those who seek to distort the opposition's theory of command responsibility and who allege that it is incompatible with the basic Liberal platform of decentralization one of whose objectives is the reduction of corruption by reducing the power of the national officials.

Mr. Kennedy is the head of the American government, which follows the decentralized system. He has shown that command responsibility is not incompatible but essential to all levels in a decentralized government. We want administrations on the national, provincial, municipal and barrio level which will be responsible for their acts and not pass the blame on to their predecessors or on to the people.

Contrary to the misrepresentations of the majority party regarding the Liberal stand, it is not the opposition's theory that a high official must go to jail for the crimes of his subordinates.

No one suggests that Mr. Kennedy be tried in court for his responsibility in the tragic Cuban miscalculation but the American President has admitted that he is morally and politically responsible and is ready to face the political judgment of the American people on this admission weighed against any corrective action which he may henceforth initiate.

Who is morally and politically responsible for the retention of tax evading cabinet officials and of other cabinet members who prosecute small tax-evaders but close their eyes to the acts of their fellow Secretaries?

We look in vain for any responsible and official stand on many vital questions — the Japanese treaty of commerce, for instance, which the head of the negotiating panel defends, the by-passed Foreign Secretary is "waitfully watching", the Commerce Undersecretary supports, the Commerce Secretary opposes, the Chairman of the Senate Foreign Relations Committee has urged "caution" on — while Malacanang is silent, undecided and not ready to command.

## 9. The Road To Greatness

### INNER WHEEL OF ROTARY
### CASINO ESPANOL, MANILA
### DECEMBER 4, 1960

The gravest obstacle to the economic development and political maturity in the country is the popular attitude of dependence which is being perpetuated by corrupt politicians through the distribution of pork barrel and social welfare handouts in exchange for political support.

There is no quick and easy road to greatness but that we must build our own road with the genius, the sacrifice, the work and the sweat not of a handful of leaders but of each and every one of the millions of our countrymen.

The kind of leadership that is needed to put the country on the right road to greatness is that which will change three things — the corrupt politician who takes advantage of his people, the people's attitude of dependence and the laws which prevent the people from helping themselves.

Too long have we allowed politicians to look upon the masses of our people as herds of animals to be conveniently led one way or the other as the political exigencies of the moment demand. At every opportunity, our people have been deceived into believing that all of our problems may be solved exclusively by the politician, and particularly by that politician who is in a position to hand out money for their roads, their schoolhouses and their pockets.

Where is the leader that is ready to lose votes, if necessary, in order to tell the people the truth? The truth is that no one can truly help the people but the people themselves. When the politician helps a certain region with pork barrel and social welfare handouts in exchange for political support, he is not really helping the people of that region. He is corrupting them. He is bribing them with their own money.

When the people need a schoolhouse, the first thing they ask is: "Who can build it for us" Where is the pork barrel that was promised to us?" In other countries, people have had the same need at stages of their national development similar to that in which our country stands today. But in those countries, the people asked instead: "Can we build the schoolhouse ourselves?" And they did. With this spirit permeating their whole attitude towards nation-building, they built strong, economically independent and politically mature democracies.

## 10. Coalitions and Principles

### SAN JUAN, RIZAL,
### JULY 23, 1959

The Progressive Party did not enter into a coalition with the Liberal Party simply to get Mr. Manahan and myself into the coalition ticket. The purpose of the coalition is to unify the opposition on all levels under honorable terms.

More important than our being in the coalition senatorial ticket is the implementation of the coalition agreement on all levels. In spite of our repeated representations, in most cities and provinces the

Liberal Party has refused to implement the coalition. Manila is only one example.

We may be united at the top but if we are disunited at the base, we cannot achieve victory. In the coming elections which are of local character, unity at the base is indispensable for victory These problems can only be settled within the coalition committee and not by the senatorial candidates. This is the reason why we have insisted on a meeting of the coalition committee. A meeting of the senatorial ticket to finalize campaign plans would presuppose that these basic problems have been settled. Since they have not been settled, we hold that such meetings of the senatorial ticket are premature.

Another reason why we consider such meetings premature is that at the last meeting of the coalition committee, the Liberal panel assured us that they would study the revision of the LP senatorial ticket with a view of strengthening it in order to achieve a sweeping victory in November. Such a revision has not yet been effected.

We are awaiting settlement of these problems in the belief that the leadership of the Liberal Party sincerely desires victory in 1959. For our part, we do not desire to abandon our men in the field who have stood by the party and its principles in its difficult years simply because we are sure of berths in the senate ticket.

-----

# XV. The State of Philippine Democracy

(Article reprinted by special permission from *Foreign Affairs* July 1960. Copyright by the Council on Foreign Relations, Inc.. New York.)

Last November, more than five million Filipinos went to the polls to vote on candidates for a variety of national and local offices. The fact itself was not news in the Philippines or abroad; Filipinos have been voting since 1906. Since 1940, however, there has been a growing truth about Philippine elections which could be news but which not even all Filipinos have come to realize: the process of elections in the Philippines is the most difficult in the world. The reason for this is to be found in a unique combination of things — a territory more challenging and a political system more demanding than those of any other working democracy today.

The Republic of the Philippines is broken up into more than 7,000 islands, of which some 400 are inhabited by the 24,000,000 souls that make up its population. While there is adequate interisland water and air transportation, land transportation in many provinces, particularly those in the Visayas and Mindanao group of islands, is far from satisfactory. Many communities in the Visayan islands of Leyte, Samar, Panay and Palawan and on the coast of the big, rich island of Mindanao can be reached only by perilous water transport. Manila newspapers, the only daily publications of national circulation, hardly ever reach these municipalities. Their isolation, once almost absolute, has lately been somewhat relieved with the increase of transistor radios distributed by government and private agencies.

Upon this rugged physical foundation there has been built a constitutional structure patterned on that of the United States. The offices and terms of office are similar except that in the Philippines members of the lower house are elected for four-year terms coinciding with those of the President and Vice President. Also, senators, of whom there are 24, are elected at large which means that the entire electorate votes for eight candidates every two years. The selection of provincial and municipal officials coincides with the senatorial elections in mid-Presidential term.

By the standards of parliamentary government, this is complex enough, but it is only the beginning of the demands made upon the electorate. Each choice for each position must be written on the ballot. Party tickets are not allowed to be posted in the polling booth, either for national or local offices. A list of all senatorial candidates, arranged alphabetically and without party identification, is all that is permitted. In the last elections, which were in mid-Presidential term, the voter who wished to choose a full ticket had to write in the names of eight candidates for senator, one for provincial governor, one for provincial vice governor, three for members of the provincial board, one for municipal mayor, one for vice mayor and ten for municipal council — a total of 25 names.

To aid the voter's memory, each party distributes sample ballots in the last days of the campaign and on election day. In this crucial period, the campaign shifts from the "battle of issues" to the "battle of sample ballots." The ability to carry these sample ballots to the barrios or villages where the bulk of the votes is found is, of course, of decisive importance in a national candidate's bid for victory.

It is not difficult to imagine the weight of the party machine in such a test of strength. The two established parties are protected by a singular electoral statute which in effect provides them exclusively with government-paid poll-watchers, who form the ready-made base for a political machine. By virtue of this privilege, the two major parties have access to the smallest, most remote village free of charge. But in the highly centralized political structure of the Philippines, the advantage enjoyed by the party in power in such an electoral system requires in every instance an almost super-human effort if it is to be overhauled.

# Faith in the Filipino

In every election the opposition has had to call for a national crusade rallied behind a figure prominently successful at capturing the imagination of the people. In 1953, the opposition Nacionalista Party was almost ready, it seemed, to officiate at the interment of a graft-ridden Liberal administration; it nevertheless found it necessary to "steal" from the Liberals their Secretary of Defense, Ramon Magsaysay, who had just set his countrymen's hearts afire by breaking the back of the Communist rebellion. With Magsaysay as their presidential candidate against an ailing opponent (the incumbent President Quirino), and with the aid of a massive citizens' non-partisan drive (the Magsaysay-for-President Movement), the Nacionalistas succeeded in overcoming the majority advantage and returning to power.

To the Britisher, the Frenchman, the Indian or the Australian, who under the parliamentary system has never experienced having to vote for a candidate on a nation-wide basis; to the Vietnamese, the Indonesian or the Malayan, whose electoral system is apt to be so simplified that in some instances he has merely to deposit in a basket a ball whose color corresponds to that of his favorite party; to the American, unaccustomed to voting for senatorial candidates at large and secure in the decentralized ambiance of his constitutional system — to all these the workings of the Philippine political and electoral system must be quite shocking. To them, the hope of any independent candidate or group of candidates being able to challenge such a system successfully must appear absurd. But to the Filipino, who is unaccustomed to admit the inevitability of the merry-go-round of the established parties, such an idea could conceivably occur.

In 1959, indeed, a group of young politicians, belonging to the two established parties and the new Progressive Party, joined in a Grand Alliance and challenged the system. They presented eight candidates for senator and a number of aspirants for local positions. They were in effect putting the electorate to the most difficult test of maturity and independence to which any democratic nation could be subjected today.

The results, in terms of a quick victory, were not sensational. A few local candidates won but no senate seats were gained. Viewed nationally, however, the showing of the senate ticket was revealing and refreshing. Machineless, fundless and almost completely watcherless, the top aspirants of the group obtained 1,700,000 votes, or about a third of the number of registered voters who actually cast their ballot. They were less than 200,000 votes behind the man who won in eighth position.

A parallel movement on the local level, the Citizens' League for Good Government of Quezon City (the official, though partial, capital of the Philippines, on the outskirts of Manila), was even more successful. The League presented six candidates for the ten-man city council.

**Raul S. Manglapus**                                                    **102**

# Faith in the Filipino

Among them were a former Secretary of Justice in the Magsaysay and Carcia cabinets, one former and one incumbent university president, a former ambassador and an Annapolis-trained former naval officer. All six came in on top and are now in control of a superbly functioning city government.

The test was difficult, but it was passed. It was a somewhat more sophisticated test than that to which most peoples in this part of Asia are subjected. This should be cause for elation for our people and for anyone else who may feel a sense of participation in the development of our democracy. It is consoling that, while we can afford to worry about such problems as decentralization and the facilitation of a freer evolution of the two-party system, the problem for others around us is a far more elementary and agonizing one — the decision, in the face of exasperating political and economic crises, whether or not to stay within the barest framework of constitutional democracy.

## II

This distinctive position enjoyed by the Philippines in Southeast Asia could not have come about by accident. Neither is it a recent twentieth-century phenomenon. The first national revolution in colonial Asia was launched by the Filipinos against Spain in 1896. Whether this was primarily because Spanish colonial policy was one of the very harshest, historians cannot agree. But one thing cannot be disputed: in 1896, only the Filipinos, of all colonial subjects in Asia, found themselves sufficiently a nation to assert their right to independence in a full-dress revolution.

There had been, of course, many regional uprisings, Ilocanos in Northern Luzon, Pampangos and Tagalogs in Central Luzon, Boholanos in the Visayas, all afire with the impatience of the Malay but not yet quite a nation, these had been separately challenging Spanish rule since the sixteenth century. There also were frustrated rebellions against the British, the French and the Dutch in other Asian lands. But what was it that hastened the maturing of Philippine nationalism so that fully 50 years ahead of all others in Asia it erupted into a successful revolution and a constitutional republic?

For this the Spaniards themselves would, paradoxically but perhaps not without reason, now like to take credit. They have argued that in 1893 the Philippines was the most economically advanced and most Westernized country in Asia. Even Filipino economic historians would admit a basic truth in this. The operations of foreign merchants (mostly British and American), which the Spaniards allowed in the country in the nineteenth century, put ready cash into the hands of the Filipinos. One of the important results was that there arose a Filipino middle class which began to demand educational and political reforms

# Faith in the Filipino

and finally provided the intellectual leadership for the revolution.

But middle-class leaders must have a nation to lead. If economics must be credited for stimulating the formation of a middle class, where lies the credit for spreading the formation of the nation? As Arnold Toynbee has noted, "The Philippines are unique in having a North American as well as a Spanish chapter in their history — unique and also lucky, because Spain and the United States are complimentary to one another as representatives of different elements in the Western Christian civilization." He credits Spanish Christianity with hastening the fusion of Filipino nationhood, and, moving further into the twentieth century, credits our American experience with contributing to what he calls "Filipino optimism." He does not find it necessary to mention that when the Americans arrived, the Philippines were in the act of inaugurating a full-dress republic, founded on a constitution duly enacted by convention.

If mention of this is unnecessary in an analysis of Filipino nationhood, the allusion does help us to start off on the right foot in evaluating Philippine-American relations. The Spanish Army, cornered in the Walled City of Intramuros for the most part by the Filipino army, chose, in order to save its pride, to surrender to the American General. This is an essential bit of history that the fair-minded American of today should consider in pondering the beginnings of Philippine-American intimacy. Another is the fact that two years later ambassadors of the Philippine Republic pleaded in vain for recognition by the world powers, including the United States, and pleaded just as vainly to prevent the signing of the Treaty of Paris which transferred Philippine territory to the United States for $20,000,000.

But the American of the late nineteenth century, no less fair-minded, we must presume, than his mid-twentieth-century counterpart, had obviously a much more limited choice of alternatives in the field of big-power-small-power relations. Assuming President McKinley's justification of "protection" to be valid, assuming the presence of a colony-hungry German navy outside Manila Bay, what action was available to effect this protection? President Eisenhower today can invoke "aid" to build the country economically, "mutual security pacts" to protect it from preying imperialists. But McKinley, living in a less progressive age and caught in the fever of empire that had contaminated his own nation, had a much poorer alternative: outright occupation.

Against this setting fashioned by the play of nineteenth century forces the performance of both Filipinos and Americans must now be judged.

# Faith in the Filipino

## III

No one, not even the "political transmission" writers of the Communist Party, dare suggest to the Filipinos today that their experience with the United States did not bring with it a substantial measure of training in the art of republican democracy. The constitutional forms and establishments which the political orator would now swear to defend with his life arc mostly copies of American institutions, not suddenly adopted on the eve of independence but introduced early in the occupation and absorbed, at times painfully, over a period of almost 50 years.

When the Philippines became a republic in 1946, her democracy was a going concern. The middle class that had gotten its start in the last century of Spanish rule had considerably expanded, a strong civil service (later to be weakened by patronage incursions) was ready to provide administrative continuity, a respected group of elders headed an independent judiciary, and the country had behind it a tradition in the separation of powers. It had just gone through an intense ten-year period of training in outright presidential democracy in the transitional "Commonwealth", which was interrupted by the Japanese occupation. For 40 years it had been prepared for tlie presidential system which was later to give it a stability enjoyed by few others in Asia. At its inception, the Second Philippine Republic, still the first in colonial Asia, enjoyed an advantage quite unique in this area: It knew where it was going. And this is why even the most acid critic of America would now grant that her administration of Philippine affairs was "benevolent".

But it is in the economic field that our American experience is today stripped bare and subjected to the most meticulous and merciless scrutiny. Granted all the personal liberty, the early suffrage, the universal education, the political stability — of what use is all this when the masses of our people were maintained in their historical status of "hewers of wood and drawers of water"? Did not the United States merely perpetuate our colonial economy, keeping us as providers of the raw materials for her giant industries, enriching a few sugar barons and coconut exporters but subjecting the millions to continued serfdom?

Charges such as these are not infrequently to be read in the press or heard on the floor of our Congress, openly or in thinly veiled insinuations, particularly in debates on attracting foreign capital. Spoken in a period of intense reexamination of our economy and feverish planning for industrialization, they are not to be dismissed as leftist demagoguery.

The Payne-Aldrich Traffic Law of 1906 was the cornerstone of Philippine-American economic relations. More than that, it set the pattern for Philippine economic development. For the free-trade relationship which it established naturally encouraged the cultivation of technical crops for absorption in the American market. With the high income from the export of sugar, copra, hemp, lumber and minerals, the Filipinos were able to import all their consumer requirements free of tariff from the United States. The result was, of course, a continuation of the agricultural economy of the Spanish era. Anyone who dared put up an industry for consumer products had to compete with the quality, tariff-free, mass-produced imports from America. And American investors found no incentive for putting capital into an area where they could readily and with less risk sell goods manufactured at home.

The Payne-Aldrich Law has been defended on the ground that it was enacted at a time when no one, not even the Filipinos themselves, could definitely tell whether the Philippines was headed for ultimate statehood, "dominion status" or independence. It is pointed out that some American states, like Montana, remain largely un-industrialized suppliers of agricultural and mineral products for general or industrial consumption in other States of the Union. There is something to be said for this defense. As late as 1941, some Filipino political and economic leaders (who would now consider themselves ardent nationalists) were agitating for a "realistic reexamination" of the independence question.

However, by successive executive pronouncements, the United States as early as 1906 was already committed to eventual Philippine independence. It would seem that American preparation of the country for political independence is not to be matched by her performance in preparing it for economic self-sufficiency. However, a few considerations are here in order.

It is not too difficult to tear down an old political structure and build up a new one. This the Americans did, when they supplanted the Spanish colonial system with a new political order. It is not as easy to tear down an old economic structure. For this is usually rooted in land-holdings, in the social complex, in such less tangible things as family relations, superstition and tradition.

Furthermore, just as our cultural optimism and political stability arc not simply the marks of our race but are also the products of many centuries of paradoxical forces, and just as we did not achieve by chance our now-victimized civil service, neither is it an accident that today we can boast of the widest entrepreneurial and technical base in Southeast Asia. In fairness, this must be attributed in substantial measure to the impact of universal education, introduced by the Americans to a people already gifted with a forward cultural outlook.

Again, the encouragement of agriculture per se does not necessarily mean developing a colonial economy. The successful industrial development of free nations, the most notable recent example of which is Australia, has invariably begun with successful agricultural development which provided both the foreign exchange and the raw materials for native mills and factories. What gave agricultural economy its colonial tinge was its combination with free trade. Once free trade ceased or was modified, the beneficent, nay, indispensable effect of agriculture on industry immediately became evident. High in the priority list prepared by our National Economic Council are those industries which process locally grown or mined raw materials. And of course, our foreign exchange reserves are to a great degree generated by our agricultural and mineral exports.

Indeed, a fairer criticism would seem to be not that there was too much emphasis on agriculture but that there was not enough. Huge tracts of land remain uncultivated and there is little scientific farming on those that are cultivated. This condition may be traced in part to the American quota system which offered no encouragement to produce more than could be admitted to the United States duty-free. But it must also be traced to other things, such as the tenancy system, which is just now emerging from its semi-feudal state.

In 1937 a joint Preparatory Committee on Philippine Affairs was created by the Philippine Commonwealth and the United States government in order to correct, before independence in 1946, the inadequate situation brought about by free trade. Before its recommendations could be implemented, the Pacific War broke out.

The devastations of war, of course, compounded the economic difficulty. To the problem of trade reorientation was added one of higher priority — rehabilitation. With the help of U.S. War Damage payments, reconstruction was largely completed by 1950 and the country entered into a period of development and limited industrialization. Adjustment to termination of duty-free relations with the United States is currently taking place through the instrumentality of the Bell Act, as amended by the Laurel-Langley Agreement.

Due to their stubborn resistance, the Filipinos suffered the greatest damage among all Japanese-occupied peoples in the war. They also have been subjected to Tammany-style travesties on the democratic process by some of their politicians. In spite of this they have managed to stay ahead of most of their neighbors in a material sense and have made spectacular gains in their struggle for readjustment and economic expansion. Between 1949 and 1957 over 13,700 new manufacturing firms were registered, and the boomlet in industrial promotion has just began. Food production has kept ahead of population increase. Exports have also increased accompanied by a noticeable rearrangement in the export trade. Sugar, dessicated coconut oil, cigars, scrap and filler tobacco, pearl buttons and canned pineapple in 1940 constituted 60 percent of total domestic exports (excluding gold and embroideries), valued at 221 million pesos. In 1957 they formed only 30 percent of the total, worth 853 million pesos. The most vigorous postwar growth in the export sector was manifested by copra, logs, lumber and base metals. A wider distribution of foreign trade has reduced United States purchases of Philippine exports from a prewar 75 percent of the total to 52 percent in 1957. Japanese and Northwestern European purchases have accounted for most of the balance.

The pace of industrialization is reflected in the curve of consumer goods imports. In 1949, they constituted 47 percent of total imports, valued at 1,172 million pesos. In 1957, they went down to 22 percent of a total of 1,129 million pesos. On the other hand, capital goods went up from 10 to 20 percent and raw materials from 43 to 58 percent.

An indication of the consistent record of Philippine growth is the country's sustained position as third highest in recorded annual per capita income among all the ECAFE countries (stretching from Afghanistan in the west to Japan in the northeast). She is surpassed only by highly industrialized Japan and rubber-rich Malaya.

Yet much more must be done — not in the vague future but as soon as resources allow. The lives of millions in the provinces have as yet been hardly touched by economic development. An urgent drive to provoke Philippine capital into leaving bamboo safes and entering productive enterprises is succeeding. It has become so popular that Congress is preparing regulatory measures, patterned after American legislation to prevent abuse. And last April, in answer to demand of private business for relief from foreign exchange controls, the administration decided to introduce partial decontrol on non-essential and non-governmental items.

But Philippine capacity to form capital is limited. Our needs and wants, on the other hand, appear unlimited. And we cannot afford to save from present consumption the resources required to realize all of them. The way out of the vicious circle is foreign capital.

## IV

In 1959, the "Filipino First" policy was born as a campaign slogan of the majority party. While it did not succeed in saving from defeat national candidates favored by the administration — even with the help of a split opposition -- the concept had some justification.

Its justification is found primarily in the preeminent position held by the more than half a million Chinese in the distributive trades, in village retailing and urban finance just as their countrymen do in varying degrees in Indonesia, Thailand, Vietnam and other Southeast Asian countries It is this situation which prompts us to continue recognizing Nationalist China rather than to give a Red Embassy in Manila a chance to coerce a ready-made economic empire into subversive action. The problem is so big that it cannot be considered simply in economic terms but in terms of national security.

Communists and extremists have tried with some success to give the policy an anti-American twist. Those who would use it for the laudable purpose of reducing the economic power of the Chinese population are denounced as blind Sinophobes, and the people are reminded that the real enemy is American imperialism. The administration was faced with the necessity of dissociating itself from this Communist propaganda and at the same time making sure that its policy did not collide with its proclaimed desire to attract American and European capital.

One manifestation of its concern over these problems was the recent celebrated case of the President's unsolicited invitation to the United States to base missiles in the Philippines. While the invitation received immediate popular support, some saw it as a patent effort to dispel any fears that the administration might be weakening in its firm policies regarding national security. Encouraged by the wide acceptance of this sudden action, the President has since then made several public statements urging a sobering of the "Filipino First" movement. In this he shows signs of following in the footsteps of other Asian countries, notably India, which have sheared off extremist nationalist fringes in order not to impede national development and the requirements of international economics. This is particularly evident in the matter of attracting foreign capital. The trend has, of course, disconcerted the Communists, whose aim has been to discourage foreign investments in Asia and thus prove the incapacity of free enterprise to give sufficient relief to underdeveloped economics.

There is also a growing awareness of the accomplishments of U.S. Government lending agencies, though the recent "Buy America" condition has not made local industrial promoters happy. Many of these find European and Japanese capital equipment better suited to their requirements. Moreover, the move has slowed down the trend toward a fairer appreciation of American intentions in Asia.

Some concern is also expressed here and in other Asian capitals over the dubious attitude taken by the United States towards the proposal to internationalize foreign aid and lending among non-Communist nations. Such a move would eliminate the fear of "Colonialism" which continues to haunt the political outlook of former dependent areas and hampers their development. There are obvious legislative, diplomatic and cross-accounting difficulties in the scheme which must be threshed out among the donor nations, but a firm statement by the United States in general support of it would have the same effect as, say, an unequivocal statement against colonialism in

# Faith in the Filipino

Africa — a renewed confidence in American free-world leadership.

In his recent book "Democracy Is Not Enough", John Scott takes a hard look at the underdeveloped lands of Asia and prescribes a sort of moratorium on democracy in order to permit them to concentrate on lifting their living standards. The Philippines is one of the countries he would exclude from this radical prescription, along with India, Japan, and Malaya. It would be more useful, perhaps, to consider them as examples to inspire rather than as exceptions to be envied. In any case, whether or not the Philippines will continue as one of the pace setters will depend on how far the current stirrings in favor of fundamental changes in our political structure can carry. The shape of our country in the years to come is being fashioned in this generation by citizens who have learnt the secret of permanent and rapid political and economic development — namely, the maximum participation of the people.

The most promising economic program will fail unless the people contribute their optimum output to its realization. Communist China knows this and is attempting to raise output forcibly by such monstrous methods as the communes. In India, dedicated men like Jayaprakash Narayan are seeking to reawaken in the Panchayats the self-reliance of the Indian villager, thereby to refashion Indian polity on indigenous bases. In the Philippines, the barrio revolution begun by Ramon Magsaysay has matured into private and official movements to revive the spirit of bayanihan, the original unwritten rule of village self-help which had been buried under the mass of initiative-robbing positive law descended from the national government, colonial and independent alike. The ultimate success of democratic Asian nationalism will come when the Indian way and the Philippine way — alike in being the way of free, voluntary initiative — arc able to demonstrate conclusively that liberty, justice and Cod need not be jettisoned in order to allow the people to work for the satisfaction of their temporal wants.

Meanwhile, because of our over-centralization, our electoral system, the many faults of our constitutional structure, it could be said that in the Philippines we may not have democracy at its best but we do have democracy at its hardest. Such a judgement, while critical of the system, is a tribute to the people. The important thing is that it is democracy and that it is working. And in the irrepressible optimism of the people and their deep-seated faith in the superiority of free enterprise lies a promise that here democracy will someday be at its best Herein lies our claim to the understanding and support of free nations.

-----

**Raul S. Manglapus**　　　　　　　　　　　　　　　　**110**

# XVI. Reform Program

*Mr. Manglapus contributed substantially to the form and content of the following:       The full text of the mani-festo outlining a statement of principles and a common program of administration ratified by the Liberal Party which paved the way for the affiliation in the official opposition of the leaders of the erstwhile Progressive Party:*

### FAITH IN THE FILIPINO

A proposal to the sovereign people by the united opposition under the Liberal Party for the re-awakening of the nation, and the redirection of its energies towards the acquisition and enjoyment of the substance of freedom by every Filipino.

### THE STATE OF THE NATION

Ours has always been, and still is, a nation-immeasurably rich in natural resources.

These resources can support a population three or four times the size of ours, at a much higher standard of living than we at present enjoy.

The development of these resources could give full and rewarding employment, right now, to every able-bodied man and woman in the Philippines willing to work.

We are equally rich in human resources. Given the chance, the Filipino is as capable as anyone else in the world of hard work and achievement, of winning a bright future for himself and his children.

Yet what do we see?

Millions of our people unemployed.

Millions more underemployed.

Other millions employed in work whose wages can barely keep them and their families alive.

We see widespread poverty and privation.

Something is wrong. Something is very wrong.

A change is not only necessary; it is urgent.

This change must begin with a change in administration.

We must do away with an administration that has failed the trust the people placed upon them.

An administration that has not only neglected to develop our national patrimony, but has misused and dissipated that patrimony.

An administration which uses power to keep the people in political and economic bondage:

# Faith in the Filipino

First, by graft and corruption in public office on a fantastic scale, unparalleled in our history;

Second, by economic and fiscal policies which it has had the effrontery to call "nationalistic," but which are in reality directed solely to the enrichment of the few who enjoy the friendship and intimacy of its high officials.

Our people are losing faith in their future; in their nationhood; in their democracy; in themselves. Unless we vote a change now, they will lose this faith altogether.

This, then, is what is at stake in this election. Our future. Our democracy. Our nation itself.

### A NEW LEADERSHIP

What is needed to restore the faith of the Filipino people?
A new leadership.

A leadership endowed with the moral qualities of sincerity, integrity, and self-sacrifice;

And which has, besides, the trained intelligence to grasp and solve the immensely complicated problems of a nation in transition to modernity such as ours.

These are the qualities of leadership which the united opposition demands of the men who are to lead the country and restore the faith of the Filipino.

### RESPONSIBLE LEADERSHIP AND COMMAND RESPONSIBILITY

The new leadership will assume full responsibility for the condition of the state and the conduct of government.

It will not seek to evade responsibility for the malfeasance of one official by attempting to dissociate itself from the perpetrator.

Neither will it cover up by pointing to another official who may appear to be performing his duties.

Our constitution provides that the President, and no one else, is the Executive. All other officials of the Executive Department exercise delegated authority and are mere extensions of the President's personality.

Therefore, while he may not be held criminally or legally responsible for the misdeeds of his appointed assistants. he is not exempt from moral and political responsibility.

Therefore, the President may not retain a tax-evading cabinet member nor refuse to prosecute him for his evasion on the ground that it is not the President's own act and thus not his concern. Worse, he may not justify this evasion by pointing to the activities of another cabinet member who appears to be discharging his normal functions of seeking out tax evaders but whose eyes are strangely blind to the evasion of his fellow official.

On the contrary, for his failure to act on specific misdeeds, for failure to correct the general pattern of corruption in government and in the present case, for deliberately abetting and encouraging it by urging his cabinet members "to provide for the future," the President must stand indicted before the people.

This is the principle of COMMAND RESPONSIBILITY.

It applies to the President for the conduct of national affairs, to the Secretary for his Department, the Director for his Bureau, the Chief for his Division, the Governor for his province, the Mayor for Ids city, the municipal and barrio officials for tlieir local administration.

## THE SUBSTANCE OF FREEDOM

Of even greater consequence than these qualities of leadership are the goals which the leaders set up for themselves and the nation and the road they propose to travel to reach these goals.

The goal of this new leadership shall be to give full substance to the freedom and independence of Filipinos. This means the development of our national resources without delay or discrimination so that every citizen may enjoy his just share of their benefits. This development must be pushed through to meet the urgent needs created by the rapid increase of our population and compounded by present government mismanagement. If it is to be undertaken within the frame-work of democracy, there must be total participation in it by every Filipino, as free citizens in a democratic society, inspired by a renewed faith in himself and his capabilities.

## FAITH IN OURSELVES

Next to faith in Cod and in our nationhood the most fundamental belief required for democratic national development is the faith of the individual citizen in his capacity to contribute to that development.

The beginning of nationalism is faith in one's self, in one's ability to work with his fellow citizens in the building of the nation.

The new leadership proposes to revive this faith. It proposes to do this by proclaiming and implementing its own faith in the Filipino, in every Filipino worthy of the name, no matter how humble his social class or economic resources. It believes in a nationalism that is truly national, a Filipinism that embraces all Filipinos. It does not believe in the so-called nationalism of this administration, which extends only as far as the narrow limits of its own clique and its supporting claque.

## HISTORICAL SELF-RELIANCE

This faith is to be revived, not created from nothing.

For the Filipino used to be possessor of a genuine measure of self-confidence. This was the character of his membership in the Barangay, a community of self-help, a community which inspired self-reliance and initiative in the individual.

After the Spanish conquest of our country, far-sighted and great-souled missionaries sought to preserve the local autonomy of the Barangay. In a Synod which they held in Manila ten years after Legaspi had made it a Spanish city, they proposed that Filipinos should be allowed to govern themselves at the local level. It was a proposal that might have changed the course of colonialism for the next three centuries. But it was not heeded.

Instead, the Barangay was incorporated into a centralized structure of government, and thus, by yielding to the demands of a colonial administration, the Spanish bureaucracy began the process of the deadening of the Filipinos faith in himself. The taxes that he paid were all funneled to Manila, and he learned to do nothing for himself, waiting for every improvement of his condition from the almighty central government which held sway far, far away from his little community.

The Malolos Constitution sought to restore some of this faith and postulated, in Article 82, the existence of the primary power of self-government, taxation and administration in the local corporations.

When the Americans came, President McKinley instructed the new administrators to presume "always in favor of the small subdivision" in the distribution of powers and directed that "the Central Government shall have no direct administration except on matters of general concern."

Instead of following these instructions, the American administrators, without much resistance from Filipino politicians, proceeded in the opposite direction. Indeed, local elections were introduced. But so was a centralized administrative Bureaucracy which reduced local communities to begging for national aid — a convenient instrument for colonial administration

The Commonwealth Constitution provided the golden opportunity for liberation of our people from the chains of a colonial pattern in government. Instead, the chains were even more securely forged. The document provided politicians with an instrument for self-perpetuation by concentrating the powers of government in national officials.

## DECENTRALIZATION

To effect this liberation, it is necessary to decentralize our government.

This administration, while paying lip service to it, is against decentralization.

It does not desire to decentralize because it is enjoying to the full the graft and the many illegal and immoral benefits deriving from the accumulation of power.

It does not desire to decentralize because it is utilizing centralized power as an instrument of coercion and corruption and for self-perpetuation in authority.

It does not desire to decentralize because it does not believe in the capacity of the Filipino for self-improvement.

It does not desire to decentralize because it sees in an awakened people the loss of its political predominance.

Administration lieutenants surreptitiously fought a delaying battle to frustrate the passage of the Barrio Charter Law. Today in many parts of the country, the law's operation is being obstructed by the administration's deadening indifference to it.

Our community development program which seeks to build the initiative and self-reliance of our rural people, has been stultified, and in some instances, it has survived only with American aid because the administration has withheld funds which it had needed for the program.

## ELIMINATION OF CRAFT THROUGH DECENTRALIZATION

Widespread graft can l>e immediately eliminated by the election of a clean and responsible leadership. It can more lastingly be solved by the dispersal of power; by the removal of the temptation presented by the excessive accumulation of power in a few hands.

For, in the words of Lord Acton, "Power corrupts, and absolute power corrupts absolutely."

## ECONOMIC PROGRESS THROUGH DECENTRALIZATION

Economic development begins with the cultivation of our lands, the extraction of our wealth from the soil and its proper marketing and distribution. This means improvement of our agriculture, the building of roads, the education of our small people in modern methods, in self-help and self-improvement. Decentralization, by reviving the initiative and unleashing the energy o( the Filipino, will speed this process.

Economic take-off begins with industrialization. A successful industrial program executed in a democratic society must be accompanied with rural development to increase incomes and purchasing power thus providing the market for the products of industry.

Advocates of a "nationalistic" industrial program allied with this administration have impugned rural development as a concurrent objective of national policy. Since industrialization in a democratic society is not possible without an accompanying rural development, it is obvious that their intent is to lead this administration and our nation inevitably to resort to socialist dictatorship, to carry out industrialization by forcing the people to work for subsistence wages, to consume less than is needed for a decent existence, or, as in the extreme form of the Chinese communes, to work as slaves for nothing in anticipation of a prosperous millenium which they have no hope of enjoying.

## POLITICAL MATURITY THROUGH DECENTRALIZATION

Political maturity is achieved by education and the best political education is actual experience in self-government.

The masses of our people will appreciate and act on local and national issues much more readily when they are restored to the mainstream of the political order and are made to feel they are participants in national activity.

Government policies, both national and local, will receive more than merely passive support from the people when they have a share in their formulation. This is possible only in a decentralized government.

The only politically mature democratic societies in the world are those whose governments are not centralized.

## DECENTRALIZATION PROGRAM

Governmental powers will remain in the national government to the extent required to implement national policy and to meet local needs beyond the capacity of local initiative and autonomy.

The bulk of basic power will be restored to the people through local governments. These will be given powers of administration, policy determination, taxation and such others as are needed to provide for die optimum social, economic, cultural and political growth of their communities.

This dispersal of power will enable small communities to provide for their local needs which heretofore have been catered to by the national government through the Pork Barrel System. The Pork Barrel System will be abolished.

Public works projects will be undertaken by the National Government in consonance with the overall economic development program. Serious consideration will be given to measures which will result in the automatic release of funds for projects upon certification of the Auditor General on the availability of funds.

The power of appointing local officials shall be progressively transferred to local governments.

The Presidential power of suspension of local elective officials from office shall be reexamined with a view to preventing its abuse specially during elections.

As the process of decentralization of government power is undertaken there shall be a parallel movement to bring the national government closer to the people and speed up its action by the establishment of regional offices with powers of decision equal to those exercised by the Head of a Department.

## THE EDUCATIONAL SYSTEM

In harmony with its policy of decentralization, the new leadership will lift from the educational system of the nation the dead hand of over-centralized bureaucratic control. It will indeed be ruthless in dealing with diploma mills run solely for profit. It will insist on the government's constitutional right to supervise all schools, public and private, in order to insure minimum standards of excellence.

But it will allow and encourage individual schools and associations of schools to raise their own standards by self-discipline and self-improvement, and to plan courses and methods imaginatively and creatively, with a view to local and regional needs, within the framework of a sound and stimulating autonomy. It will certainly put a stop to the tendency of the present administration to impose on the schools of the nation, by poorly devised and even more poorly administered compulsory examinations, the unanimity of the graveyard.

An earnest reexamination of our educational goals and values shall be undertaken with a view to making our educational system responsive to the needs of a modern society, particularly in respect to education for science.

## ECONOMIC DEVELOPMENT

In consonance with our faith in the individual Filipino, the new leadership is pledged to an economic program that will bring about prosperity for all and achieve the ultimate goal of placing control of the national economy in Filipino hands by releasing the energy of every enterprising Filipino freely to create wealth.

# Faith in the Filipino

In place of restrictive, stultifying and self-defeating economic controls, it pledges to provide positive guidance and incentive in the form of tariff policies designed to consolidate our national economic gains; credit preferences that will open up leading economic sectors to sustain economic growth; and stable economic policies.

Economic policy shall be liberated from the arbitrary, high-handed and personalized procedures which, under this administration, promotes not economic growth but unmitigated abuse of political power.

Vigorous steps shall be taken to restore economic freedom under the enduring stimulus of the market economy. This will be accompanied by a revision of the tariff code to provide necessary safeguards for free enterprise. This tariff code shall be made to operate in place of the control powers now exercised by the Central Bank.

Further measures shall be undertaken for the protection of products of Filipino industries in the domestic market.

Government policy must support this program of free enterprise by reducing the practice of public borrowing to the following minimum prerequisites:

(1) That the government should borrow only for the capital investment requirements of clearly productive and self-liquidating projects; and

(2) It should borrow at the "going" cost of money, i.e. "free enterprise" involves allowing interest rates to seek their own level.

It will adopt fiscal and credit measures that will sustain a stable currency and diminish excessive pressures on foreign exchange reserves.

In brief, the new leadership will place the development of our economy primarily in the hands of private enterprise. The national energy will be concentrated on economic activity, wealth creation and making profit through honest toil on the part of the citizens. The government will refrain from competing with private capital; on the contrary, it will be ready to assist the businessmen by helping provide needed credit and continually creating a favorable climate for investments.

The new leadership will solve unemployment and under-employment through effective Incentives to private enterprise and a massive public program of non-inflationary productive and labor-intensive projects. Immediate action shall be taken to develop the areas which, because of their resources and their underdeveloped state, offer prospects of maximum economic gains such as Mindanao, Sulu, Palawan, the Cagayan Valley, and others.

## ACRICULTURE AND MINING

The Philippines is blessed with vast agricultural resources that must be developed and scientifically exploited not only to provide immediate employment and increased earnings to the great majority of our people, but also to achieve maximum productivity.

The rural income shall be increased in order to provide a marketing base for the products of local industry. As a corollary to this objective, the education and training of our rural people in self-help and self-reliance through the community development program and allied activities shall be given massive, unequivocal support. To this end, the administrative machinery to carry out this program shall be given a legislative charter and protected from the inroads of politics.

Local agricultural production must complement the needs of our industries for raw materials; it must keep pace with the rate of increase in overall population growth as well as the increasing rate of urbanization.

Our agricultural production is the solid and lasting prop to the long-run effort to industrialize the economy. Agriculture, therefore, cannot be neglected in favor of "insulated" industries that are dependent upon imported raw and semi-processed materials which create very limited employment opportunities.

The new leadership proposes sustained government support to our export agricultural production in the form of independent credit facilities, free importation of agricultural machinery unhampered by government restrictions, free solicitation of foreign credit for modernization and expansion of production, and agricultural research on plant pests and diseases, greater yield, more efficient methods and maximum utilization of agricultural products and by-products. Agricultural production for local consumption and export shall aim to maximize labor absorption not only to relieve the grave problem of unemployment but also to increase foreign exchange earnings. Conservation policies and practices shall be immediately established to put a stop to the wanton destruction and dissipation of our natural resources, such as forests and fishing grounds.

The mining industry will bo vigorously supported to the end that it may render the maximum benefits to our people at the earliest possible time. Undue tax and financial burdens as well as red tape, regulations and controls which hinder the speedy and efficient exploitation of our mineral resources shall be done away with.

## INDUSTRY AND COMMERCE

The ultimate economic goal of the new leadership is the industrialization of the national economy in order to absorb the millions of unemployed and underemployed.

Determined and coordinated efforts shall be made to redirect Filipino industrialization towards the organization and establishment of "impact" industries, that is, industries that will set off a chain reaction leading to progressive and cumulative growth of the national economy. Government credit preferences and direct government assistance and guarantees to investment in "impact" industries shall be provided.

Close attention shall be given to proposals for regional foreign trade and commercial arrangements, always with the objective of fostering our industrializing economy.

The government will provide incentives and support for Filipinos going into commerce, both domestic and international, so that our trade shall, as soon as possible, be under Filipino control.

## CAPITAL MOBILIZATION

The new leadership pledges to mobilize, through definite incentive policies, the sizable hoards of capital now idle in the vaults of private banks, in government credit institutions and in households.

It will provide reasonable guarantees to private capital investments in productive industries in which the prospects of profits are low and the risks of failure are great.

Definite and consistent policies aimed at the attraction of foreign capital to supplement local capital resources shall be formulated by way of encouraging joint ventures and guaranteeing protection, reasonable profit margins, and repatriation of profit and capital.

## GOVERNMENT CORPORATIONS

Government corporations have been misused by this administration for political patronage and for institutional extortion from the people of funds for political campaigns and personal enrichment.

Their continued existence would be contradictory to the new leadership's commitment to private enterprise.

Government should refrain and withdraw from all enterprises which private capital is capable of undertaking by itself.

All government enterprises that do not discharge this pioneering function or essential public services shall immediately be liquidated or turned over to private hands.

## CAREER PUBLIC SERVICE

By immoral example, by indiscriminate use of political patronage, by indecision, by cronyism, this administration has sapped the government service of its creative energy, dedication and efficiency.

The leadership believes in the capacity of the Filipino for honest and intelligent public service. But the bankrupt policies of this administration have prevented the exploitation of this capacity in three ways:

First, competent men are repelled by government employment;

Second, trained, experienced and competent civil servants are driven by frustration into leaving the service;

Third, potentially valuable civil servants stagnate, developing passive attitudes, thus obstructing the implementation of public policies.

The new leadership will reverse this process by example, by prompt decision, and by pursuing the quest for competence through selection and advancement on the basis of merit and achievement.

To this end, it will establish the following training centers:

An Executive Academy to train a corps of senior civil servants for appointment or promotion to responsible positions;

Management Institutes, maintained by local governments with assistance from the Executive Academy, to develop city, provincial and municipal executives and staffs;

A Foreign Service Academy, whose graduates shall have exclusive right to appointment to the corps of Foreign Affairs Officers.

The new leadership will provide vigorous and sustained support to all management improvement agencies of the government.

Sound management practices shall replace political expediency in the conduct of governmental affairs.

## FOREIGN AFFAIRS

By its barefaced corruption, now a matter of wide international knowledge, this administration has dragged our national prestige down to incredible depths.

By its indecision and disregard of international sensibilities, this administration has made of our foreign service the object of ridicule in diplomatic councils and disgraced our people in the eyes of the world particularly of our Asian neighbors.

This administration has made the brash claim that its foreign policy is based on national self-respect. The opposite is evident. At no point in our history has the Filipino travelling abroad ever felt the sense of shame that he now feels when confronted with the evidence of his country's disgrace.

The new leadership, by this proposal for a re-awakening, redirection and consequent national self-fulfillment, will rehabilitate this fallen prestige and substitute for this sense of shame a feeling of pride in being a Filipino.

It is thus that it proposes to strike for this nation a confident and unequivocal posture in world affairs.

The primary justification for foreign policy is the national interest. In the present context of world events, the first objective of this policy should be the national security.

To this end, the new leadership will confirm this nation's adherence to the principles of collective security and of mutual defense. It will cooperate with the United States of America and other free nations in the pursuit of these principles.

It will support the United Nations and its agencies as the greatest single hope of peace in our time.

It recognizes international Communism as the gravest external and internal threat to national security, as well as to individual liberty and dignity.

It declares itself unequivocally against Communism and renounces neutralism as an unrealistic, purposeless and irresolute stand in the face of the world wide assault on freedom directed from Moscow and Peiping.

It will take an unhesitating position and assume the initiative in favor of self-determination by all people and the liberation of subject nations from all forms of colonialism.

It will utilize foreign policy to expand the country's international trade and support Filipino entrepreneurs in this field.

## CULTURAL DEVELOPMENT

The new leadership has faith in the richness and greatness of Filipino Culture.

It recognizes that the Malay base of this culture has been enriched by Hindu, Islamic, Christian, Chinese, Spanish and Anglo-Saxon influences.

While facing and taking pride in the fact that the great majority of our people are participants in the great Christian tradition, it will give commensurate attention to the development of the culture of our minorities.

Particular attention shall be given to enabling our Muslim population to discharge in dignified collaboration with their Christian brothers their functions as members of the Filipino nation and enjoy their just share of the national leadership.

To foster cultural research, development, promotion and exchange, there shall be created in the Department of Education the position of Undersecretary for Culture whose office shall coordinate all government cultural agencies and activities and shall assist private initiative in this direction.

## RESPONSIBLE CITIZENSHIP

The way out of stagnation and into sustained economic social and political growth is individual hard work, sacrifice! and self discipline.

The new leadership does not wish to deceive our people that it can be otherwise.

On the contrary, it is its purpose by example to spur our people to undergo those painful changes in attitudes, values and motivations which are necessary for this growth.

The new leadership shall, by administrative action, by legislation and constitutional amendment, by public policy, by official and social recognition, by education and persuasion seek promptly to place the Filipino in a position to meet this historic opportunity to build for himself a sturdy and vibrant society.

The new leadership envisions this Filipino taking moderate imaginative risks in his strivings; postponing some short-run gains in favor of larger and more lasting benefits taking personal responsibility for his decisions and his acts-displaying a social conscience and a sense of history; believing in his God, in his country — in himself.

## FAITH IN THE FILIPINO

Here is the Key to Our Nation's Future.

-----

# APPENDIX

Mr. Manglapus' oration "Land of Bondage, Land of the Free" was delivered in December, 1939 at the Ateneo Auditorium. He was representing the Ateneo de Manila in a national inter-university oratorical contest sponsored by the Civil Liberties Union of the Philippines. President Manuel L. Quezon was guest of honor and Senator Lorenzo M. Tahada, then President of the CLU, was chairman.

Mr. Quezon was so impressed by the oration that thereafter he called upon the young orator to give him advice whenever he was to deliver an important speech.

A reproduction of the oration as printed in 1939 for special presentation to Mr. Quezon is found in the following pages.

**o LAND OF BONDAGE**
**o LAND OF THE FREE**

**RAUL SEVILLA MANGLAPUS, A.B.**
**Ateneo de Manila**

-----

**To His Excellency Manuel L. Quezon, President of the Philippines, Defender of the TAO, this defense of the TAO...**

-----

# UNITED STATES OF AMERICA
# COMMONWEALTH OF THE PHILIPPINES

---------o---------

## IN THE HIGH TRIBUNAL OF CIVIL LIBERTIES

MIGUEL LOPEZ DE LEGAZPI, adelantado of Spain, 1565,
SINIBALDO DE MAS, secret investigator for the Spanish Crown, 1840,
THEODORE JAGOR, archaeologist for the Berlin Museum, 1859,
JOHN FORMAN, American trader, 1924,
KATHERINE MAYO, volunteer American investigator. 1925, and
JIM MARSHALL, Correspondent-at-large, 1938, PLAIN-TIFFS,

### vs.

The TAO of the Philippines, DEFENDANT.

--------o--------

### COMPLAINT

Come now the plaintiffs in the above entitled case and to this honorable tribunal of civil liberties respectfully allege

That the said *Tao* is guilty of ignorance, improvidence, refusal to comply with health regulations, non-support of family, gambling, indolence, vice, non-cooperation with the government.

Contrary to **temporal and eternal** laws.

Wherefore, we respectfully pray that the said *Tao* be condemned to loss of citizenship and be deprived of the rights enumerated in Article Three of the Constitution.

Your Excellency,
Mr. Chairman
Fellow Speakers,
Ladies and Gentlemen.

My client, the defendant in this case, has admitted that the charges in the complaint just read against him are in great part true. But before you pass judgment upon him, I pray you hear his story:

Once upon a time, the *tao* owned a piece of land. It was all he owned, but he cherished it, for it gave him three things, having which he was content: life, first of all, and liberty, and happiness.

Then one day the Spaniard came and commanded him to pay tribute to the Crown of Spain. The *tao* paid tribute. And he was silent — because in his simple but passionate trust in the promise of the *informacion posesoria,* he was certain that he was still master of his land.

Now the Spaniard did not send the tribute to his king, but kept it for himself; and in this way he became rich. And with riches evil entered into him, and he came to the tao a second time with a formidable document, and said: "According to this *decreto real*, which unfortunately you cannot read, this that you have been paying me is not tribute but rent, not *tributo* but *canon,* for the land is not yours but mine. The *tao* paid the *canon* and said nothing ... He ceased to be a freeman. He became a serf. Still the *tao* held his peace. The *canon* went up and up. The *tao* starved.

And this time at last he spoke. Not in words, but with that rustic instrument with which he cleared the land once his own — the *bolo.* He transformed it from an instrument of tillage to an instrument of death, and with it he drove out the stranger. Then he returned to his field saying: "Now, indeed, shall I again he master of this land, once my own, but stolen from me by the trickery of quicker wits than mine."

But the *tao* was wrong. For the land indeed had another master; but it was not he.

And the new master was not a stranger, but his own countryman grown rich. And the tao had a new name, *kasama,* which to us means partner, but which to the *tao* meant still a slave, for once more he suffered from his countryman the same things he had suffered from the stranger: the rents, the usury, and all the rest of it. And so he remains today; for this story has no happy ending; or if it has, that ending is not yet.

Yes, the *tao* returned to his field thinking that he was free. So did you, ladies and gentlemen, so did everyone of us think that the *tao* was free, when he was given a constitution, when he was given a Bill of Rights to guarantee his freedom dearly won!

You are familiar. I am sure with the provisions of the Bill of Rights?

NO PERSON SHALL BE IMPRISONED FOR DEBT.

NO LAW SHALL BE PASSED ABRIDGING THE FREEDOM OF SPEECH.

THE LIBERTY OF ABODE AND OF CHANGING THE SAME WITHIN THE LIMITS PRESCRIBED BY LAW SHALL NOT BE IMPAIRED.

NO LAW GRANTING A TITLE OF NOBILITY SHALL BE ENACTED ...

By the way, you are acquainted also, I imagine, with that equally interesting document — I mean, the Bill of Wrongs? It is the obverse, I believe, the rather disreputable unwritten rider to the Constitution, which renders the Bill of Rights nugatory with regard to the *tao*. For instance:

NO PERSON SHALL BE IMPRISONED FOR DEBT. That depends on what you mean by a prison. If you mean by a prison those comfortable apartments of temporary detention now so much the fashion, where a man for the trifling cost of performing some misdemeanor (as for instance. murder) is guaranteed a bed to sleep in, regular meals, band concerts, the movies, the radio — if you mean by a prison all this —then I regretfully admit that the *tao* is free. But I mean by a prison no such palatial residence. I mean by a prison something very different — a two-room shack, rent by every wind, without any comforts, except that three families have there the privilege to starve. That is the *tao's* prison. Its doors, if you can call them such, are wide open. It is a prison none the less. For the *tao* is bound to it, not with chains of steel, but with a stronger chain than that — his honor. No man knows this better than the man who put him in that prison — the usurer. To the *tao* who comes to the usurer for money, the usurer says: "Here is money. But after the harvest you must pay me double and in kind." And then the harvest comes. The usurer takes it all for he fixes the price of the harvest. It is a beautiful system, ladies and gentlemen. It is called *takipan* — its most beautiful virtue being that it keeps the *tao* in perpetual debt. There is on record in the Bureau of Lands the example of a man who borrowed ninety pesos from a usurer. Having in the interval of nine years paid one thousand four hundred pesos on the debt, he still owed at the end of nine years one thousand six hundred pesos! What a pity, ladies and gentlemen, that the *tao* is an honorable man. I have no doubt at all that that man continued to pay his debt — and that his children, still imprisoned in the same shack where their father starved and died, are paying that debt to this day.

And yet, ladies and gentlemen, the *tao* is constitutionally' free.

NO LAW SHALL BE PASSED ABRIDGING THE FREEDOM OF SPEECH. If you mean by law, the statutes officially passed by an officially empowered assembly representing the *tao* then I say we have no law abridging the freedom of speech. But there is another kind of law — a statute unofficially passed by an unofficial assembly, a one-man assembly, where the *hacendero,* representing himself proposes the law to himself, and himself approves it; a statute, not promulgated in the Official Gazette, but secretly in the barrios, before election time, a statute, not sanctioned by the courts of justice, but by the swift injustice of ejection and starvation in the streets. This law has only one provision:

# Faith in the Filipino

"I have a candidate. He has little faults (for instance, embezzlement), but see that you speak well of him. See that you say nothing evil of him — that you vote for him, or else ..."

The *tao* complies. So would you, ladies and gentlemen, if the penalty was destitution.

And yet, this man is 'constitutionally' free!

THE LIBERTY OF ABODE AND OF CHANGING THE SAME WITHIN THE LIMITS PRESCRIBED BY LAW SHALL NOT BE IMPAIRED. And what are the limits prescribed by law? A line running from west to east along or near the twentieth parallel of north latitude, and through the middle of the navigable channel of Bachi, and thence a line enclosing these seven thousand pearls set on a silver sea, these seven thousand spots of earth, these Isles of the Philippines, the habitation of a free people, blessed by a kindly sun, this demi-paradise swept by the very winds of Eden, and thence along the one hundred and eighteenth degree meridian of longitude east of Greenwich to the point of beginning. Nay, more than that, — the *tao* may go beyond this imaginary enclosure — the world is his — and if he should decide to pack up his belongings and settle on the moon — the law of the nation cannot stop him. But the law of the *hacendero* can and does stop him that law by which he is tied like an animal by the chain of indebtedness to two hectares of unproductive earth enclosed by a line running from one *mojon* of the last cadastral survey to another, a spot of earth, a very little spot of earth — the habitation of a slave! Can he leave it? Certainly he can. He can cast off this debt, this usurious debt, this debt saddled on him from time immemorial. He can do this and then sneak away into exterior darkness, dragging his carabao with his children on his back. But will he? No, ladies and gentlemen, he will not, because the *tao* is an honorable man.

And yet, this man is 'constitutionally' free!

NO LAW GRANTING A TITLE OF NOBILITY SHALL BE ENACTED. Of course not. Why should the *hacendero* come crawling to the National Assembly for titles of nobility? He is a noble — by his own decree. He can step into his carriage — supercharged — and be conveyed to his ducal castle in Pampanga and there mete iron justice to five hundred slaves. You are acquainted with his coat-of-arms — a vulture, couching on a scarlet field, with the motto — OMNES PROPTER UNUM — all for one — and, by the way, that one is I! You will not find this escutcheon engraven in any wall. You will find it engraven by the brand of perpetual serfdom in the heart of the *hacendero's* slave — your brother in blood — the *tao*! Is this not the part of a noble — that while the Conde de Negros, Duque de Muscovado, Baron von Coprax is flicking up a richly-liveried foot to the mad boom of the Conga in some air-conditioncd pavilion, the slave ofhis feudal household broils in the blistering sun that he may leave money to squander! Is this not the part of a noble to inveigle a freeman into his service with golden promises; to call him friend, *compadre,* partner, KASAMA, and then with a wave of the magic wand of usury, to transform him into a slave?

And yet, ladies and gentlemen, the *tao* is constitutionally' free!

No wonder, then, that the *tao,* being a slave, has acquired the habits of a slave. No wonder that after three centuries in chains, without freedom, without a hope, he should lose the erect and fearless posture of the freeman, and become the bent, misshappcn, indolent, vicious, pitiful thing he is! Who dares accuse him, who dares rise up in judgment against this man, reduced to this subhuman level by three centuries of oppression. Ladies and gentlemen, the *tao* does not come here tonight to be judged — but to judge! Hear then his accusation and his sentence:

I indict the Spanish *encomendero* for inventing taxes impossible to bear!

I indict the usurer for saddling me with debts impossible to payl

I indict the irresponsible radical leaders who undermine with insidious eloquence the confidence of my kind in our government!

I indict the *hacendero* for seizing my lands by subtle trickery and reducing me to peonage! I indict him for sacrificing the honest efforts of an honest government on the altar of his illimitable greed!

You accuse me of not supporting my family. Free me from bondage and I shall prove you false!

You accuse me of ignorance. But I am ignorant because my master finds it profitable to keep me ignorant. Free me from bondage, and I shall prove you false!

You accuse me of indolence. But I am indolent not because I have no will, but because I have no hope. Why should I labor, if all the fruits of my labor go to extinguish an unextinguishable debt! Free me from bondage, and I shall prove you false!

Give me land. Land to own. Land unbeholden to any tyrant. Land that will be free. Give me land for I am starving. Give me land that my children may not die. Sell it to me, sell it to me at a fair price, as one freeman sells to another and not as a usurer sells to a slave. I am poor. But I will pay it! I will work, work until I fall with weariness for my privilege, for my inalienable right to be free!

But if you will not grant me this last request, this ultimate demand, then build a wall around your homes ... build it high! ... build it strong! ... place a sentry on every parapet ... for I who have been silent these three hundred years, will come in the night when you are feasting, with my cry and my bolo at your door. And may Cod have mercy on your soul.

---oOo---